Collection Development:
Cooperation at the Local and National Levels

SALALM Secretariat
Memorial Library
University of Wisconsin--Madison

COLLECTION DEVELOPMENT: COOPERATION AT THE LOCAL AND NATIONAL LEVELS

Papers of the Twenty-Ninth Annual Meeting of the
SEMINAR ON THE ACQUISITION OF
LATIN AMERICAN LIBRARY MATERIALS

University of North Carolina
Chapel Hill, North Carolina
June 3 - 7, 1984

Barbara G. Valk
Editor

SALALM Secretariat
Memorial Library, University of Wisconsin--Madison

ISBN 0-917617-10-X

C O N T E N T S

PREFACE

The report of the President's Commission on Foreign Language and International Studies was issued in November, 1979, culminating years of research. Among its findings, the report recommended the creation of a national plan for the cooperative acquisition and cataloging of foreign area collections. Three years later, a plenary session was held at SALALM XXVII in Washington, DC, to investigate the implications of this recommendation for Latin American studies. Panelists reviewed the status of cooperative programs in the United States and, in the face of declining library budgets, proposed strategies for implementing a national level program.

The 1982 SALALM XXVII panel determined that although great strides had been made in recent years to develop regional and national level library networking systems, the most notable achievements had been in the area of technical services, such as shared cataloging programs and the expansion of bibliographic utilities. It was therefore both timely and appropriate that John Hébert, President of SALALM and then Deputy Chief of the Hispanic Division of the Library of Congress, should focus attention at SALALM XXIX, in Chapel Hill, North Carolina, on the other vital component of library cooperation, collection development. His goal for the Seminar was to encourage an exchange of information and ideas among theoreticians and practitioners concerning a wide range of issues involved in cooperative collection development, and from this to begin to derive new priorities for acquisitions and strategies for resource sharing.

The theme of the Seminar was developed through a series of panels and workshops which yielded the papers in this volume. The first group of papers is drawn from three theme panels treating (1) the history of Latin American library development and the development of Latin American studies programs in the United States; (2) the status of national level cooperative acquisitions programs; and (3) cooperative collection development within a single research library. A fourth paper, on cooperative collection development efforts at a regional university in the Caribbean area, results from a workshop on that topic. Together, the papers present an overview of the history of of Latin American studies in this country as well as current cooperative collection development problems and practices at the local and national levels.

The papers in the second group are the product of a panel on Latin American legal resources, an important but highly specialized field of research and collection development about which many Latin American bibliographers are largely unfamiliar. Included is extensive information about current research trends in Latin American law, the range and uses of available research resources, techniques for identifying and acquiring legal research materials from Latin America, and the use that is made of those materials by legal researchers in the United States.

The next section focuses on the collection and organization of two other specialized types of library materials: manuscripts and photographic sources. Finally, the foreign acquisition field trip as a collection development technique is examined from both American and British perspectives, and its effectiveness is evaluated in an analysis of survey results.

Following the Seminar papers is a bibliography of guides and directories to Latin American and Caribbean libraries, archives, and information centers which was prepared under the auspices of SALALM by Celia and Jesús Leyte-Vidal. A preliminary version of this work appeared in the Papers of SALALM XXVII; the expanded bibliography is presented here in its entirety for the convenience of the reader.

The papers included in this volume clearly reflect the substance of SALALM XXIX but not necessarily its structure nor the full extent of the program. In some instances, panel presentations were delivered from notes and did not result in formal papers. Some workshops were structured as informal discussions for which papers were neither appropriate nor requested. Included in the volume, therefore, is a full listing of the panels and workshops given at the Seminar and their participants. Summaries of all the sessions appear in the September 1984 issue of the SALALM Newsletter. Cassette recordings of most of the sessions may be obtained from the SALALM archives in the Nettie Lee Benson Latin American Collection at the University of Texas at Austin.

Special thanks are due to the University of North Carolina at Chapel Hill and to Duke University, which jointly sponsored SALALM XXIX, June 2-7, 1984, thereby making the presentation of these Papers possible.

Barbara G. Valk
Editor

Latin American Studies and Cooperative Collection Development

1. LOS ESTUDIOS LATINOAMERICANOS EN LOS ESTADOS UNIDOS

Federico G. Gil

El surgimiento y desarrollo de los estudios latinoamericanos en los Estados Unidos ha tenido lugar aproximadamente en los últimos 75 años. Para trazar ese desarrollo es conveniente dividir este período en cuatro etapas de principios de siglo a 1920, de 1920 a 1944, de 1945 a 1970 y durante la década de los 70.

1900–1920

Las ciencias sociales en un concepto moderno se inician con la labor de un grupo de historiadores en un pequeño número de universidades entre las que se distinguen principalmente California, Harvard, Johns Hopkins, Pennsylvania, Wisconsin y Yale. Historiadores de esa primera generación de latino-americanistas tales como Bourne en Yale, Channing en Harvard, McMaster en Pennsylvania, Moses en California y Turner en Wisconsin, fueron los pioneros en el estudio de América Latina. Estaba también entre ellos el eminente historiador y bibliotecario Hubert Bancroft, fundadador de la Biblioteca Bancroft en la Universidad de California. Dos estudiosos contemporáneos de las ciencias políticas también dejaron huellas durante este primer período: Paul Reinsch en Wisconsin de 1899 a 1913 y Leo S. Rowe que enseñó en Pennsylvania de 1895 a 1917 y pasó luego a ser Director General de la Unión Panamericana durante muchos años. Otra figura importante fue Herbert Bolton, historiador de las tierras fronterizas del Oeste y California y mentor de cerca de un ciento de historiadores dedicados a la América Latina.

Entre 1900 y 1920 surgió una nueva generación de latino-americanistas. Durante ese período se concedieron grados de Ph.D. a 14 candidatos dedicados a tópicos de investigación sobre América Latina. Entre ellos estaban figuras como William Spence Robertson de Yale, el geógrafo Hiram Bingham (descubridor de las ruinas de Machu Picchu) y tres discípulos de Bolton: Charles Chapman, Herbert Priestly y Charles W. Hackett.

Todas las obras relacionadas con la América Latina publicadas durante el período anterior a 1920 fueron de índole histórica con excepción de unos cuantos trabajos de carácter geográfico o económico. El enlace hacia la entonces incipiente ciencia política lo constituían dos elementos: la historia diplomática (orientada hacia las relaciones internacionales), e historias legalísticas e institucionales de las instituciones coloniales españolas y un poco más tarde de los experimentos constitucionales en la América

Latina durante el siglo XIX. Para 1920 ya se habían publicado unos 13 libros y 10 artículos de significación. Dos de estas obras tuvieron especial impacto: South America de James Bryce, que fuera embajador de la Gran Bretaña en Estados Unidos, y Latin America de Francisco García Calderón. Esta última obra fué por mucho tiempo considerada el estudio clásico del ambiente político latinoamericano.

1920-1944

El segundo período se caracteriza por un incremento notable en el número de grados doctorales obtenidos por candidatos dedicados al estudio de la América Latina. De un total de 72, 15 fueron producto de la Universidad de California cuyas actividades se veían favorecidas por la proximidad geográfica a la cultura latinoamericana, la riqueza de materiales de la Biblioteca Bancroft, y la dinámica presencia de Herbert Bolton. Otras universidades que comenzaron a ganar prestigio en el campo de estos estudios fueron Illinois, Texas, Chicago, Duke, y Clark, además de las mencionadas con anterioridad. Entre las principales figuras de esta generación se encuentran los historiadores J. Fred Rippy (California), A. C. Wilgus (Wisconsin) y Arthur P. Whitaker (Harvard); los estudiosos de las ciencias políticas Russell H. Fitzgibbon (Wisconsin) y J. Lloyd Mecham (California); el sociólogo John Gillin (Harvard), y el antropólogo Charles Wagley (Columbia). Durante este período es que se despierta el interés hacia la América Latina por parte de los estudiosos de la ciencia política y comienzan a aparecer estudios sociológicos y de antropología social, estos últimos especialmente en las universidades de Chicago, Columbia y Harvard.

Se pueden citar aproximadamente 60 obras importantes publicadas durante este período. En su mayoría, fueron publicadas por editoriales universitarias que comenzaron a ganar prestigio e importancia durante la década de los 30. Pronto se distinguieron dos en especial, las de la Universidad de California y la Universidad de North Carolina. Esta última inició la publicación de una serie de obras históricas de prominentes autores latinoamericanos traducidas al idioma inglés.

Debe mencionarse que durante esta etapa en el desarrollo de los estudios latinoamericanos, comienzan a surgir los estudios sobre política latinoamericana caracterizados, como era de esperarse dado el desarrollo de la ciencia política en aquel momento, por su naturaleza descriptiva, legalista e institucional. Estos estudios, sin embargo, sentaron sólida base para los estudios posteriores, que siguiendo nuevas corrientes de la ciencia política, dedicaron su atención, con objetivos más prácticos, a la dinámica política y al análisis de procesos y actores políticos.

Es oportuno mencionar que, a pesar de algunos esfuerzos meritorios, el estado actual de los estudios sobre política latinoamericana en esa región siguen caracterizándose por un énfasis legal, filosófico o histórico. Tal como sucedió en Estados Unidos, y hasta época reciente en Europa, los estudios de la política en América Latina, herederos de una excelente tradición legalista hispánica, siguen manifestando una fuerte tendencia a mantenerse aislados de la realidad, dedicando su atención principalmente a los aspectos formales de instituciones y procedimientos. En cierta medida, la literatura política de Latinoamérica consiste por una parte de estudios jurídico-filosóficos, ciertamente valiosos pero de utilidad limitada para el conocimiento de la vida política, y por otra parte de un vasto número de libros y panfletos de tono polémico de muy escaso valor científico. Por eso decimos que el estado actual de la Ciencia Política en los países latinoamericanos es comparable con la situación de dicha disciplina científica hace cincuenta o sesenta años en los Estados Unidos y en Europa. Aunque hasta ahora hay que lamentar que los esfuerzos hacia enfoques funcionales hayan sido en su mayoría obra de estudiosos extranjeros, ya existen indicios, como veremos más tarde, de una saludable corriente hacia la promoción del estudio científico de la fenomenología política.

1945-1970

Los estudios internacionales y los idiomas extranjeros experimentaron un desarrollo verdaderamente espectacular a partir del fin de la Segunda Guerra Mundial. Como consecuencia del conflicto, los Estados Unidos asumieron una posición predominante entre las potencias industriales mientras su conocimiento de otras naciones y de otras culturas era relativamente deficiente. Tanto su población como su economía experimentaron un dramático crecimiento durante el cuarto de siglo que siguió al conflicto mundial. Paralelo a este crecimiento tuvo lugar un extraordinario aumento en el estudiantado universitario, debido en gran parte a leyes como el famoso G.I. Bill que impartieron beneficios sustanciales para aquellos veteranos de la guerra que deseasen adquirir una educación superior. Los efectos de esta legislación sobre los estudios latinoamericanos fueron notables. El número de grados doctorales (Ph.D.s) con énfasis en la región se multiplicó en todas la ciencias sociales. En el campo de la ciencia política de 1945 a 1963 fue especialmente notable. Las 113 tesis doctorales escritas durante ese período sobre política iberoamericana fueron producto de 29 universidades. Las cuatro universidades que encabezaron la lista fueron California (Berkeley), North Carolina, Texas y California (Los Angeles).

La percepción por parte del liderazgo político y educacional de la apremiante necesidad de crear y difundir conocimiento sobre otras áreas del mundo tuvo como consecuencia la inversión de grandes recursos económicos. La fundación Ford estableció en 1952 el Programa de Becas para el Estudio de Areas Extranjeras (Foreign Area Fellowship Program), bajo cuyos auspicios un número considerable de especialistas en Latinoamérica han completado sus estudios e investigaciones de campo. El mayor aporte económico fue suministrado por el gobierno federal mediante la legislación conocida como la Ley Educacional de Defensa Nacional (National Defense Education Act, NDEA), promulgada en 1966. Con anterioridad a esta iniciativa gubernamental, la comunidad académica había respondido a las necesidades nacionales con el establecimiento en 1946 del Comité de Investigaciones de Areas Mundiales (Committee on World Area Research) por el Consejo de Investigaciones en las Ciencias Sociales (Social Science Research Council). En 1948 se fundó la Asociación de Estudios del Lejano Oriente (ahora llamada Asociación de Estudios Asiáticos [Association of Asian Studies]) y en 1956 se fundó la Asociación de Estudios Africanos (Africana Studies Association). Finalmente, en 1966 se fundaron la Asociación de Estudios del Medio Oriente (Middle East Studies Association) y la Asociación de Estudios Latinoamericanos (Latin American Studies Association, LASA).

El resultado de estos esfuerzos, que rindieron fruto durante estos veinticinco años, fué el sorprendente aumento en el número de especialistas en todas estas áreas, de programas al nivel de post-grado y de cursos ofrecidos por universidades, así como la instrucción en estudios de área a los niveles primario y secundario del sistema educacional.

Según Richard D. Lambert, habían en 1971 en Estados Unidos 13,139 no-estudiantes especialistas en estudios de área, y 7,177 alumnos matriculados en un programa universitario de estos estudios. Los datos reunidos más tarde por Lambert muestran que en 1979 los Estados Unidos tenían casi 20,000 especialistas en áreas extranjeras garduados de universidades.* De este número, aproximadamente un 20% eran especialistas en América Latina.

Un gran número de colleges y universidades instituyeron en su curricula los programas que se conocen como Estudios Latinoamericanos, aunque algunas instituciones prefirieron los términos Estudios Hispanoamericanos o Iberoamericanos. Otras instituciones se especializan en los llamados Estudios Luso-Brasileros o simplemente Brasileros. El término "Latin American Studies" implica un "énfasis" o "concentración" al nivel subgraduado (undergraduate major), y al nivel de maestría (Master) o doctorado (Ph.D.). Existen las siguientes variaciones en estructura programática:

1. La existencia simplemente de una comisión o consejo encargado de adquirir los materiales de investigación y estudio de las bibliotecas o el asesoramiento de aquellos estudiantes interesados en Latinoamérica.

---

*Richard D. Lambert, "Language and Area Studies Review," Monograph 17 (Philadelphia, PA: American Academy of Political Science, 1973).

2. Un programa de cursos, al nivel de subgrado (under-graduate), integrados en forma tal que el alumno puede obtener un énfasis concentrado sobre América Latina al mismo tiempo que un "major" en los campos tradicionales.

3. Un programa de estudios de área en el que el estudiante puede escoger su "major" (campo principal de estudios) o su "minor" (campo secundario de estudios) sobre Latinoamérica.

4. Un programa de estudios de área conducente a la obtención de un título graduado o quizás un certificado; algunos solamente permiten un Master of Arts (M.A.) (Maestría); otras sin establecer el Ph.D. (doctorado) permiten, sin embargo un "minor" (concentración secundaria) en estudios de área, pero un "major" (énfasis central) en una de las disciplinas o campos tradicionales.

El debate entre aquellos partidarios de los estudios de área y aquellos otros que sostenían la superioridad del adiestramiento en los campos tradicionales comenzó en la década de los 1940 y ha durado muchos años. Mientras unos mantenían los méritos del enfoque tradicional, otros arguían la necesidad de un alto grado de especialización. Entre las universidades de mayor prestigio, Stanford University bajo el liderazgo de Ronald Hilton mantuvo hasta 1964 el enfoque de área en programas de postgrado. En la actualidad, la tendencia que predomina es la que favorece el adiestramiento en uno de los departamentos tradicionales (historia, ciencia política, sociología, etc.) con especialización adicional sobre Latinoamérica. Al nivel de maestría (M.A.) existen programas que añaden a dicho diploma una certificación en estudios latinoamericanos mediante el cumplimiento de requisitos adicionales. Al nivel del doctorado (Ph.D.), generalmente no se expiden certificados, aunque en su mayoría dichos programas de postgrado son lo suficientemente flexibles como para permitir un número considerable de cursos o asignaturas relacionadas con la América Latina de carácter interdisciplinario.

La mayoría de los programas de estudios latinoamericanos con una amplia base institucional, tales como Texas, North Carolina, Florida, Columbia, New York University, Tulane y California (Los Angeles), se han organizado bajo institutos o centros. En la Universidad de Carolina del Norte (Chapel Hill) por ejemplo, existe el Instituto de Estudios Latinoamericanos desde 1940, que funciona como instrumento de coordinación y enlace entre todos los departamentos que ofrecen cursos sobre Latinoamérica y tiene profesores especialistas en el área. Sirve también de centro de información coordinador de todas las actividades universitarias de todo tipo que tengan relación con América Latina, y actúa también como organismo administrador de diversos programas de investigación, estudio o adiestramiento. Algunos de estos centros o institutos tienen publicaciones periódicas y auspician monografías y estudios bibliográficos. Muchos de estos centros han recibido en el pasado aportes económicos considerables por parte de fundaciones privadas como Ford, Rockefeller, Carnegie, Kellogg, Tinker, etc. Algunos deben su creación a la legislación federal denominada National Defense and Foreign Languages Act (NDFL).

En su mayoría, estos centros existen en universidades de importancia aunque se encuentran algunos en "colleges," instituciones de menor tamaño y sin programas de postgrado. Algunos centros importantes, como el Centro de Tenencia de la Tierra (Land Tenure Center) de la Universidad de Wisconsin, son producto de contratos con agencias gubernamentales de asistencia internacional como la Agencia para el Desarrollo Internacional (Agency for International Development, AID) y se dedican a determinados aspectos técnicos de investigación en América Latina.

A medida que se mutiplicaron los programas de estudios latinoamericanos, se hizo mas obvia la necesidad de coordinar esfuerzos a un nivel nacional. Se crearon entonces los organismos regionales para estudios latinoamericanos, como, por ejemplo, la Conferencia del Sudeste en Estudios Latinoamericanos (Southeastern Council on Latin American Studies, SECOLAS). La Fundación Hispánica de la Biblioteca del Congreso publicó el primer Directorio de Latinoamericanistas, y comenzó sus actividades el Comité de Estudios Latinoamericanos (Latin American Studies Committee) del Consejo de Investigaciones de Ciencias Sociales (Social Science Research Council). Un extraordinario paso de avance lo constituyó la creación de la Latin American Research Board, que auspició la Revista de Investigación Latinoamericana (Latin American Research Review, LARR) que comenzó a publicarse en el otoño de 1965. Entre las universidades miembros fundadores de dicha revista trimestral, hoy día órgano oficial de la Asociación de Estudios Latinoamericanos (Latin American Studies Association, LASA), se encuentran las instituciones más prestigiosas del país.

De 1970 hasta el presente

Para finales de la década de los 60, los Estados Unidos disponían de un crecido número de excelentes centros de estudios de área, con expertos altamente especializados y provistos de bibliotecas adecuadas, responsables por una notable producción en la investigación científica. Este auge de los estudios internacionales se debió parcialmente a una crisis internacional: el lanzamiento de "sputnik" por la Unión Soviética y la consiguiente reevaluación de las necesidades científicas y educacionales que confrontaba el país. Superada esa experiencia, se inició otro período caracterizado por un gran desinterés público y un fuerte sentimiento aislacionista, productos esencialmente de la gran desilusión sufrida con la traumática experiencia de la guerra de Viet Nam. Esta situación, como era de esperarse, se ha reflejado en el campo de los estudios latinoamericanos. De por sí, estos estudios siempre han tenido un carácter cíclico en el sentido que

su auge o decadencia ha sido marcado por ciertos eventos internacionales determinantes de cambios en la política exterior de los
Estudos Unidos. Así, por ejemplo, dichos estudios tendieron a
prosperar en la década de los 30 durante la "Política del Buen
Vecino" del Presidente Roosevelt, dictada por la depresión económica mundial; durante el período de la Segunda Guerra Mundial
por necesidades estratétgicas; y, más tarde, durante el breve
período de la Alianza para el Progreso del Presidente Kennedy,
producto esencialmente del reto a la hegemonía norteamericana en
el hemisferio que representó la Revolución Cubana. A estos
períodos siguieron siempre otros durante los cuales decayó el
interés público y gubernamental en América Latina. Desde el fin
de la década del 60 se ha entrado en un nuevo ciclo de decadencia y la escasez de recursos ha sido causa de la inactividad de
algunos centros de estudio de área así como del éxodo de algunos
especialistas hacia otras áreas críticas como el Sudeste de Asia, el
Medio Oriente y Africa.

No cabe duda que en estos momentos los estudios latinoamericanos en los Estados Unidos atraviesan una crisis y que la
atención del gobierno y de organismos privados, a pesar de los
acontecimientos en Nicaragua, El Salvador, Guatemala y otros
países del Caribe, tiende ahora a centrarse en el Medio Oriente y
en la región del Golfo Pérsico, principalmente a causa de la crisis
energética.

BIBLIOGRAFIA

Bennett, Wendell C. Area Studies in American Universities.
New York, NY: Social Science Research Council, 1951.

Davis, Harold E. Social Science Trends in Latin America.
Washington, DC: American University Press, 1950.

Glade, William P. "Problems of Research in Latin American
Studies." University of Texas, 1979. Mimeo.

Gómez, R. A. The Study of Latin American Politics in University
Programs in the United States. Tucson, AZ: The University
of Arizona, 1967.

Goodman, Louis Wolf. "Latin American Studies in the United
States: National Needs and Opportunities." Working Paper
No. 37. Washington, DC: Latin American Program, The
Wilson Center, 1979. Mimeo.

Hall, Robert B. Area Studies. New York, NY: Social Science
Research Council, 1947.

Lambert, Richard D. "The Lambert Report"--"Language and Area
Studies Review." Monograph 17. Philadelpha, PA: American
Academy of Political and Social Science, 1973.

Moreno, Frank J., and Rodman C. Rockefeller, eds. "Social Research in Latin America." The American Behavioral Scientist, 7:1 (Sept.), 1964.

President's Commission on Foreign Language and International Studies. Strength through Wisdom: A Critique of U.S. Capability. Washington, DC: U.S. Government Printing Office, November, 1979.

Roett, Riordan. "Institutional Development and Language and Area Studies." Baltimore, MD: The Johns Hopkins School of Advanced International Studies, 1979. Mimeo.

Steward, Julian H. Area Research. New York, NY: Social Science Research Council, 1950.

UCLA Center for Latin American Studies. Guide to Latin American Studies. Los Angeles, CA: UCLA Latin American Center Publications, 1966.

Wagley, Charles. Area Research and Training. New York, NY: Social Science Research Council, 1948.

Wagley, Charles, ed. Social Science Research on Latin America. New York, NY: Columbia University Press, 1964.

2. NATIONAL LEVEL COOPERATION, COOPERATIVE COLLECTION DEVELOPMENT PROGRAMS, AND THE RESEARCH LIBRARIES GROUP

Deborah L. Jakubs

In 1982 I spoke on "The Sharing of Collection Responsibility," a topic that is closely related to the present discussion.* Then, as now, I was concerned about the mechanism for cooperation among libraries and about the need to develop a common language to describe our Latin American collections. I am pleased to say that there have been important changes since 1982. The Research Libraries Group (RLG) conspectus has continued to evolve and is now on the verge of being adopted by many libraries as part of the Association of Research Libraries (ARL) National Collections Inventory Project (NCIP). The draft conspectus worksheets for Latin America have gone through several incarnations, and as of this writing are in the last stage of preparation for their official sanction by fall of 1984. Once SALALM has approved the worksheets, data collection can begin and we will be on our way to a national inventory of Latin American collections. Data will be carried at RLG in the "Conspectus On-line" and will be accessible to anyone with an RLIN search account.

The RLG conspectus, briefly, is an overview, or summary, of existing collection strengths and future collecting intensities (in other words, the present state of the collection and the policy for future collection) in each area. Conspectus data have been collected for RLG institutions and the Library of Congress in subjects representing about 80 percent of the LC classes. Arranged by subject, class, or a combination of these (not strictly tied to the LC classification scheme), the divisions of the RLG conspectus contain standardized codes that describe collections on a scale of 0 (out of scope) to 5 (comprehensive). Language codes can be used to further qualify a collection level. Subject bibliographers evaluate their collections using the conspectus worksheets as guidelines, assigning levels and, if relevant, language codes. Notes, either large (called "scope notes") or small, are permitted, for example, to report on a special collection or an area of focus within the collection. Reported data are fed into the "Conspectus On-line," an

*Deborah L. Jakubs, "Sharing Collection Responsibility and the Problem of Database Compatibility," Public Policy Issues and Latin American Library Resources: Papers of SALALM XXVII, Washington, DC, March 2-5, 1982 (Madison, WI: SALALM, 1984).

interactive RLIN database developed in 1982, and can be searched in many ways--by subject, collecting levels, institution, or a combination of these. The "Conspectus On-line" was a major step forward and enhances the usefulness of the data tremendously. It can manipulate data in ways that were not possible when the information was stored only in paper format.

The question I would like to raise in this paper concerns the uses that will be made of the conspectus data: How will the data fit into our goal of developing a national plan for shared collecting responsibilities? Phrases such as "national inventory," "collection development on the national level," the "national sharing of collecting responsibility" have been widely used in recent years. What do we mean by these things in specific terms? My years at RLG taught me many things, not the least important of which was that theory is one thing and reality another; it is one thing to have an idea and quite another to implement it. Developing a functioning national system of shared collecting responsibility has many steps, and most of them are taken slowly. It is in this context that we must regard the conspectus now, as we prepare to collect data on Latin American collections.

The conspectus must serve one purpose for RLG and another for SALALM. Within RLG, which is a formal partnership, the conspectus is the primary tool for carrying out the work of the main standing committee, the Collection Management and Development Committee. Filling in conspectus worksheets is for bibliographers at RLG institutions both an exercise in getting to know their collections and a serious step toward consortium-wide cooperation. We in SALALM may see the conspectus in the same light, but is it really the same?

RLG has a formal mechanism for guaranteeing some degree of cooperation on the national level. This takes the form of the "Primary Collecting Responsibility," or PCR. Agreeing to accept a PCR in a given field indicates a research library's commitment to buy material to maintain a level 4 (or research-level) collection in that field. PCR assignments are based on collecting levels as reported in the conspectus, and accepting a PCR is taken very seriously. It is formalized in writing and signed by the library's representative to the RLG Board of Governors. PCR commitments may be used in the library's dealings with the university administration to defend acquisitions budgets in a given field, based on the interest of the RLG partnership as a whole. What sort of mechanism can SALALM create to guarantee adherence to an agreement to accept a PCR or PCR-substitute? What kinds of commitments do we need and can we have?

An anecdote about PCRs illustrates just one of the problems we must confront. At RLG I spent a great amount of time on the telephone. One day I was speaking with a librarian at a well-known New England institution which participates in RLG

programs but is not at present a full member. The subject was
the Law conspectus. We discussed the worksheets and various
related subjects for some time, until finally the person flatly
admitted that his institution would prefer to accept PCRs for all
areas of law. I was astounded (especially since the data for
other institutions were barely beginning to arrive) and asked him
the reason for so magnanimous an offer. His response was that
his institution did not trust other institutions to collect at the
"research level," since that could mean many things to many
people. He believed that their own level 4 could be of
considerably higher quality than that of some other institutions.
This illustrates the elusive factor of trust among institutions, and
it underlines the need for specific guidelines to ensure that we
are all speaking the same language, so we can confidently accept
that a level 4 means the same thing to all concerned.

With regard to the enforcement of a cooperative system,
another difference between the SALALM and RLG contexts is that
RLG members have a well-developed automated interlibrary loan
(ILL) system underpinning the Shared Resources Program and
functioning in support of cooperative collection development. As
we know, the key to ensuring success in a cooperative collection
development venture is access. Through the RLG/ILL system,
blue-label UPS service is guaranteed, ensuring that patrons will
have the requested materials in hand within just a few days, if
not sooner. There is no charge within the partnership for this
service.

How does the question of access fit into our plans in
SALALM for national-level cooperation? Can we justify to patrons
the fact that we may be relying on another institution for a
needed item and counteract the impression that the library is
cutting back service or emphasizing acquisitions in one area at
the expense of another? How can that all-important access be
assured? I am not suggesting that RLG has achieved the optimal
solution, nor that we should all join RLG; I am only pointing out
the context in which the conspectus was developed. To para-
phrase Dr. John Haeger, RLG's Director of Program Coordination,
the conspectus was not devised with a national collection
inventory in mind; it was designed to serve the needs of RLG
institutions (a relatively small number) in the area of cooperation,
to be sure they were speaking the same language when describing
and discussing their collections.

I do not mean to sound pessimistic. I do, however, feel
that if we in SALALM are to adopt the conspectus for Latin
American materials we must identify our purposes specifically and
use it as a tool to meet those ends. Jeffrey Gardner, of ARL,
was at Duke University recently to monitor the progress on a
Collection Analysis Project we have been carrying out. He com-
mented to me that many libraries erroneously see the conspectus
as a magic formula for automatic cooperation in collection

development. There is nothing magical about it. It is, after all, only a tool--a tool that is only as good as the uses to which it is put. We may not use it in the same way that RLG has; we cannot force all our institutions into a formal arrangement that does not now exist and in fact may not be realistic. We must assess our goals and use the conspectus to achieve them.

Despite what may be construed as a negative tone, I do believe that the conspectus can offer much to SALALM. The following suggestions of some concrete uses to which SALALM can put the conspectus are offered as a springboard for further thought and discussion. First, one of the major advantages is, of course, that it allows us to speak the same language when describing our collections. The conspectus has often been criticized for being "too subjective." As my anecdote indicated, we need to devise specific guidelines so that we are all describing a level 4--or any level--in the same terms. In several subject areas, the bibliographers who devised the worksheets have at the same time laid down a set of definitions of each level, written in terms of the type of material collected. This has worked quite well to differentiate between levels. We do not need to feel that we must complete the conspectus worksheets in a vacuum; discussion with others at work on it, comparing values assigned to subjects, is a good idea and can help to clarify ambiguities.

A second advantage is that the conspectus encourages bibliographers to get to know their collections. Feedback to RLG from collection development staffs after working on the conspectus indicates its value as a training device, as a way for new bibliographers and other staff to learn about the strengths and weaknesses within the collection and to define and describe its parameters. Filling out a conspectus worksheet is not an easy task; it is very time-consuming and requires much attention to detail. But all have generally agreed that the experience is well worthwhile. It can also result in the writing of comprehensive collection policies.

To counter the worry about subjectivity in the conspectus, I propose that we construct a verification study to be tested against the results of our data collection. RLG institutions have carried out such tests, which usually involve checking a bibliography or bibliographies against collections; in effect to verify or test the values reported. Verification studies have been applied to the conspectus in many fields; for example, English literature, French literature, Renaissance/Baroque art and architecture, mathematics, chemistry. The verification tool selected by the RLG Music Program Committee members was a shelflist measurement, so their work with the conspectus has been both qualitative and quantitative. In nearly all cases, the results of the verification studies have borne out the reported "subjective" ratings. These studies can show if an institution's reported values are out of line with those of others, and the values can then be revised.

I believe that there is some work in progress at RLG to set ranges in various subjects using the results of the verification studies. For example, if an institution has 80+ percent of the titles on a list selected for verification, it may report a level 4; if it holds 60-80 percent, a level 3, and so on. This would vary by subject area, of course. I would suggest that SALALM set up a committee or task force to compile a set of verification studies to be used for Latin American studies collections once data collection for the conspectus is underway.

Perhaps the most important use to which SALALM can and ought to put the conspectus data we are about to gather is cooperation--not yet on the national level but on the local and regional levels. A cooperative arrangement for two or more institutions is a complex feat of engineering and requires constant vigilance, guidance, and reassessment. Those involved in such ventures know that new questions always arise. Faculty need or expect things that seem unrealistic; emphases within one of the institutions may shift, and so on. I believe that if the conspectus were developed into a kind of joint collecting policy for institutions that wish to formalize cooperation, it would, in the long run, further the cause of cooperation on the national level and bring us closer to the goal of a national plan.

3. COLLECTION DEVELOPMENT WITHIN THE INSTITUTION:
THE ROLE OF THE LATIN AMERICAN BIBLIOGRAPHER
AND THE ROLE OF THE FACULTY

William D. Ilgen

In the last twenty or thirty years there has been a significant reversal in the roles played by the Latin American bibliographer and by the faculty in collection development. Until sometime in the 1950s and 1960s, the trend in American academic libraries was to consider the selection of resources as largely the prerogative of the faculty. For the most part, bibliographers were seen as expediters who received and processed faculty orders. Their role was distinctly secondary. The rationale for this arrangement was that the faculty were best qualified, by training, experience, and academic responsibility, to determine the needs of the collection. That argument, however, has in the intervening years become more and more irrelevant as libraries have grown in size and complexity, and as ever greater numbers of academically trained bibliographers have been hired by collection development departments in the nation's research libraries. Gradually, the responsibility for collection development and, therefore, for the selection of resources has come increasingly to be placed in the hands of these library area specialists.

One beneficial effect of this shifting of major responsibility for selection from the faculty to the bibliographers has been the introduction of system into what was formerly a somewhat random process. Faculty selection inevitably had to be done during time borrowed from teaching and research. Understandably, it had to be done largely unsystematically, generally on the basis of the most readily accessible dealer lists, bibliographies, or journal reviews. The area specialist, on the other hand, has been able to devote full professional attention to all the myriad tasks involved in collection development and to plan and put into operation much more comprehensive and systematic selection strategies than were possible for faculty selectors.

These strategies, as devised by the area bibliographer, are characteristically developed only after careful study of the information needs of the university community. They reflect such key factors as institutional objectives, the strengths and weaknesses of the present collections, the nature and levels of current instructional and research programs, future plans for the curriculum, and the possibilities of resource sharing with other institutions. It is only on the basis of this kind of analysis that the actual selection strategies are prepared and, subsequently, monitored and revised regularly as new circumstances arise.

Over the years, experience has shown the wisdom of this shifting of responsibilities from the hands of the faculty to those of an area bibliographer.

This is not, however, to argue against faculty involvement in the development of the collection. Faculty involvement remains as crucial today as it has ever been. Collection development in an academic setting is, by its very nature, a cooperative venture. Since the library is at the very heart of the intellectual life of a university, every member of that community, and particularly the faculty, has a legitimate stake in the quality of the library's collections. The faculty's efforts need, however, to be channeled in far more productive ways than they were in the past. The use of faculty time to select materials that are more effectively and systematically handled by an area bibliographer is patently wasteful. It is for this reason that most major research libraries today make a clear distinction between the acquisition of current imprints and readily available retrospective materials and the acquisition of less accessible retrospective, unusual, or highly specialized materials. Because the former usually constitute the bulk of a library's annual acquisitions, and because they are most easily gathered systematically, they are now regularly assigned to collection development specialists. By contrast, involvement of the faculty is strongly encouraged and readily sought in the identification and selection of the latter types of materials that may well escape the bibliographer's collection nets.

Beyond their involvement in specialized selection, the faculty can also play an indispensable consultative role in many other aspects of collection development. Indeed, if area bibliographers are to function successfully as informed collection managers, they need to be in close contact with the area faculty and to become intimately involved with them in the academic enterprise. For their part, the faculty ought also to keep themselves well abreast of the area bibliographer's work so that they will be able to provide the kind of timely advice and support that will ultimately be of greatest benefit to the collection. Because the nature of that work is so often something of a mystery to the faculty, it would be useful to review it here, if only in broad outline.

Collection development area specialists tend to play a dual role in libraries: one in technical services and one in public services. As technical services librarians they are charged with the development and management of the area collections, and as public service librarians they are required to provide specialized reference assistance to patrons. Since the focus of this discussion is on the collection development role, it alone is emphasized hereafter. It should not be forgotten, however, that the area specialist's role usually includes these other responsibilities as well.

The gathering of materials from Latin America is an arduous process, given the capricious nature of the market. Unlike most of their colleagues who work in other areas, Latin American bibliographers face a publishing universe of kaleidoscopic complexity. The product of Latin America's presses is nothing if not elusive. Indeed, the lack of adequate bibliographic control of area publications is the Latin American specialist's principal and never-ending challenge. Current, comprehensive national and trade bibliographies, the bibliographer's standard and classic primary tools for systematic selection, are universally lacking. For this reason, the Latin American bibliographer must early learn to live with a system of "nets," or checks and balances, to insure adequate coverage of current publications. In this way, if a title happens not to be identified in a first pass through an initial net of current dealer lists (almost always the timeliest sources), it stands a good chance of being caught further down the line in any one of a number of other systematically arranged bibliographic "back-up" instruments. These additional selection nets include such standard bibliographic tools as the Library of Congress proofslips; national and trade bibliographies, such as the Fichero bibliográfico hispanoamericano; specialized bibliographies such as the Handbook of Latin American Studies, the Inter-American Review of Bibliography, and the MLA bibliography; and the review listings in specialized journals such as the Latin American Research Review and the Hispanic American Historical Review. Though by no means foolproof, this system comes closer than anything else currently available to providing the Latin American bibliographer with a reliable instrument for consistent, systematic selection of area resources.

Most area specialists also make use of a number of other, secondary, sources of acquisitions. The most important of these are blanket order and approval programs, which enlist the active participation of dealers in the selection of preestablished types of materials from their areas, and gift and exchange programs. These, in conjunction with the previously described direct selection plans, are, in broad outline, the major day-to-day responsibilities of the area bibliographer.

To return, then, to the main subject of our discussion: What are the respective roles of the faculty and the Latin American bibliographer in the development of the area collection? Since, as we have seen, the question of academic training and area specialization is not really at issue, the issue becomes the best and most efficient utilization of respective professional skills in the accomplishment of the task at hand. On that premise, the broader disposition of roles seems quite clear. To the area bibliographer should go the professional responsibilities associated with organizing, directing, and monitoring the growth of the collection; to the faculty, that of ascertaining that this growth is indeed meeting the needs of study, teaching, and research in the institution. These roles ought ideally to be complementary, of course, with both the faculty and the bibliographer contributing from greatest strength, and at the most appropriate and useful level; and it should be collaborative, since genuine cooperation, especially in an undertaking of this magnitude, is the only solid foundation for truly productive work.

4. COLLECTION DEVELOPMENT: THE THEORY, THE PRACTICE, AND THE PROBLEMS-- FROM THE PERSPECTIVE OF LITERATURE

María A. Salgado

The idea of focusing on "the theory, the practice, and the problems" of collection development appears at first glance to be a straightforward, well-rounded approach to a discussion of Latin American collection development and the development of Latin American Studies programs. Upon closer examination, however, the subject becomes less clear-cut. I have concluded that the "theory" part of the topic is fine: no one can possibly deny that, ideally, faculty and bibliographers, working together in peace and harmony, should be able to develop a wonderful collection. The "practice" part of the topic, however, even under ideal conditions, does not appear to function nearly as well. From the perspective of a faculty member there are too many other professional obligations that interfere with total dedication to the task of collection development. This conclusion forced me to confront the third part of the topic, "problems," which in my opinion is the major concern and the one to which I can speak most readily.

When I say that I can speak more readily to the point of "problems," I do not mean to imply a negative viewpoint. On the contrary, I feel very positive and optimistic, because the procedures have improved one hundred percent since the days, some fifteen years ago, when I first served as faculty Book Order Chairman for Spanish American literature at the University of North Carolina, Chapel Hill. At that time I had just been awarded a Ph.D. in Peninsular Spanish Literature by the University of Maryland and had joined the faculty of the Spanish Department at North Carolina. I had no concept whatsoever of the library's holdings or of the needs of the Latin American collection, and I had no idea of how to go about making amends for my ignorance. The fact that I had been trained in Peninsular literature did not seem to matter at all. With the job came tons of catalogs--or so it seemed at the time. They arrived at my desk at regular intervals with the request from the dealers to order what we needed.

At that time, the library's bibliography section for Spanish American Studies was independent from that of Spanish Studies, and so were the budgets. This meant that a disproportionately higher amount of money went to Peninsular literature. Despite the wide coverage of countries, epochs, and genres involved in the Spanish-American area, its budget was only about one fourth that of Spanish, and Spanish itself received only half of what

French received. Under the adverse conditions of an incompetent Book Order Chairman and a low budget, it is not surprising that the Spanish American holdings were not even being maintained, let alone being built for future needs.

Since those days, and contrary to Murphy's Law, the situation has definitely improved. Now the library has a joint Latin American and Iberian Bibliography section that deals with all library matters pertaining to Spain, Portugal, Spanish America, and Brazil. This has simplified considerably the procedures for ordering books and serials and for keeping up with the collection in general. At the departmental level the situation is also better. Interest in Spanish American literature has grown considerably; our budget is on a par with that of the Spanish department, and we are no longer below the French department in terms of book-purchasing power. In addition, we now have three faculty members in the area of Spanish American literature, which helps to oversee collection development in three different areas of interest.

The library's new approach to collection development is a sound one, and it has made my job as Book Order Chairperson infinitely easier. Under the present system, the flood of catalogs I used to receive has dwindled down to a trickle. My main responsibility now is to fill in gaps in the collection by taking care of retrospective orders, while the Latin American bibliographer orders directly almost all current publications. Additionally, the faculty are encouraged to advise the bibliographers (and we do notify them on a regular basis) of specific current publications in our fields that we consider essential for the collection. To be a part of the process of acquisition is very important to me, because although I trust the bibliographers and although I know they are doing a first-rate job, I am still concerned that, through an oversight, some important publication may not be purchased.

The library collection also fulfills my specific research and teaching needs in many ways. Teaching Spanish American literature is quite a different matter from teaching most other literature courses. Literature is normally understood as a discipline that is concerned with aesthetics, and aesthetics prides itself in keeping a proper distance from everyday concerns. In teaching Spanish American literature one soon discovers that everyday concerns keep interfering with aesthetics. The deep commitment of Latin American intellectuals to solve some of the basic socioeconomic problems of their countries has meant that their creative works go beyond aesthetics into the sociopolitical arena. Because of this, any teacher of Spanish American literature has to be concerned with the other disciplines included under the umbrella of the curriculum of Latin American area studies. And here, the teacher of literature has to rely entirely on the books and other materials that his or her colleagues in history and the social sciences have provided for the collection. In this regard, I have always found that the collection has satisfied my needs well.

Another problem one must face when teaching Spanish American literature is the overwhelming ignorance of the students—and in some cases of the faculty—with regard to understanding the multifaceted cultural background of the so-called Third World countries, countries that in this case, and despite their variety and different degrees of advancement and industrialization, are all commonly referred to as the "banana republics to the south." I must confess that although I cannot do much about the ignorance of the faculty, I definitely can and do do something about student ignorance. Not only do I recommend to Spanish majors that they consider a double major in area studies, I also try to indicate to other students the convenience of having at least some courses in the Latin American area. As for the students who major in Spanish American literature, I believe that in order to have a successful program, I must rely, once again, on the collaboration of the other members of the faculty and of the library, who together provide the support and fill in the gaps that cannot be overseen from my department.

I have also regularly enlisted the help of the library in providing the students with information on sources for their research papers, theses, and dissertations. I have found the personnel at the Humanities desk and at the Bibliography section, as well as at the Undergraduate Library, very willing to speak to the students, to orient them, and to help them solve specific research problems.

The other very important area in which I have always depended on the support of the Latin American collection is in my own private research. My field of specialization deals with poetry, often considered one of the most esoteric areas in literature. But here again, in Latin America, even poetry has a way of becoming concerned with problems other than aesthetics—one need only recall the poetry of César Vallejo, Pablo Neruda, or Ernesto Cardenal to realize how politically involved poetry can become. The wealth of material contained in the collection has allowed me to write on subjects as culturally oriented as the Mayan poetry of Miguel Angel Asturias or as historical and sociopolitical as the allusions of the Canto general of Pablo Neruda. In both of these cases the collection has made available to me books that I would never have thought to acquire. Additionally, the bibliographers have been very helpful to me and to my students in tracking down books when neither our collection nor the one at nearby Duke University has them available. The bibliographer is further useful in notifying me of the arrival of books on authors or areas that he knows are of special interest to my immediate research needs.

But the most important point of all, which I would like to emphasize in conclusion, is that our efforts to build a strong collection have been done well over a period of time, and in this respect I must mention the efforts of Professors Sturgis Leavitt, Sterling Stoudemire, and William McKnight. The glory of doing research in Spanish or Spanish American literature at the University of North Carolina, Chapel Hill, is that very rarely does one seek an item that is not found in the library. I often marvel at the tremendous number of items at hand in the collection, and I feel almost guilty when I realize that I will never be able to become acquainted with all of its treasures.

5. COLLECTION DEVELOPMENT IN THE EASTERN CARIBBEAN: UNIVERSITY OF THE WEST INDIES

Alan Moss

The University of the West Indies is a regional university supported by fourteen governments, with campuses situated in Mona,
Jamaica; St. Augustine, Trinidad; and Cave Hill, Barbados; and
with university centres or departments of extra-mural studies in
the non-campus countries. The Cave Hill campus is the smallest
of the three, with a mainly undergraduate student population of
around 1,500.

Elsewhere in this volume are reports of large research
collections with budgets which are sizeable, even if they are not
as large as their directors might wish. The fourteen countries
which support UWI are, however, mainly categorised as "Less
Developed Countries." The only three which qualify as "More
Developed Countries" are Jamaica, Trinidad, and Barbados, and
of these the former two are experiencing a period of severe
economic restraint. Jamaica's problems result from a falling-off in
oil revenues and the general debilitating effects of the economic
recession, and Trinidad is feeling the effects of a series of
draining currency devaluations. It is against this kind of
economic background, then, with its accompanying pressures on
budgets, that collection development at Cave Hill is considered.

The principal special collection which the Main Library at
Cave Hill endeavours to maintain is a West Indies Collection, the
functions of which are twofold: to support teaching and research,
and to serve as an archival repository for the materials collected.
This second function is a necessary one for UWI to carry out,
given the lack of good archival facilities in many of the territories
served. In scope, the aim is to be as comprehensive as possible
for the English-speaking Caribbean, with the proviso that publications from Jamaica, Trinidad, and Guyana are not collected with
the same degree of vigour as are those of the other territories,
since the university libraries which exist in those countries all
aim to build a strong local collection. For the French-, Spanish-,
and Dutch-speaking Caribbean we are much more selective,
collecting mainly in the fields of language and literature, history,
and the social sciences, in accordance with the dictates of the
teaching and research programme at Cave Hill.

In order to acquire materials for the West Indies Collection,
attempts are made to utilise the advantages given to us as a
result of our regional structure. Thus, the three main campus
libraries will collect publications from each other, not only from

the campus territory itself but from other islands to which its staff have access. Cave Hill, for instance, would try to secure for Mona and St. Augustine copies of the publications originating in the other Eastern Caribbean islands which sometimes make their appearance in the Bridgetown bookshops, while Jamaica is more likely to be able to acquire the output of the more northerly of the territories in which we are interested. Clearly a certain amount of duplication may occur, but this is felt to be preferable to missing the opportunity to acquire a title which may not stay in print very long.

We attempt to make use of the presence of extra-mural tutors in the countries served by the university by seeking their assistance in the acquisition of local publications. While the immediate response is invariably good, it has proved difficult to achieve a sustained performance. Doubtless a more sustained performance on the part of the library in reminding them of the kind of assistance we would like to receive would go some way toward improving the situation.

With a regional university there is inevitably a certain amount of travelling to be done to accomplish its work. The effort is made to let such travel serve double duty as collecting trips as far as possible, but unfortunately the person travelling is not often the person best qualified to make the collecting trip, and so the results are not as satisfactory as they might be. In order to circumvent this difficulty the libraries have tried and continue to try to obtain funds specifically for collecting trips, which are seen as the only way to ensure that our collections are as complete as we would wish them to be. Regretably, these efforts have not as yet met with significant success. The "restructuring" of the university, which was scheduled to come into effect on 1st August 1984, by means of which the individual campuses will have greater autonomy in some respects, may well result in a reduction of inter-campus travel, and will therefore make the matter of funds for collecting trips even more critical.

The regional nature of the university would appear to have worked against us recently when a decision was taken to withdraw the status of legal depository from the Main Library at Cave Hill and also from the main campus library in Jamaica. The intention was to retain the Barbados Public Library as one depository and to add the Barbados Department of Archives as a second, the latter two being more obviously "national" institutions, in comparison to UWI. In passing, I would like to draw attention to a very welcome, and in my experience unusual, feature of the new legal deposit legislation, which requires printers to inform the legal depositories on a quarterly basis of work which they have done. This provision will certainly ease the task of the depositories in tracking down material which should have been lodged with them but which has not been, either through negligence or ignorance.

We have been looking so far at the collection of materials available within the Caribbean, but we are also concerned to make available in Barbados materials which at present exist only in foreign repositories, chiefly governmental records in the Public Record Office in London but also legislation of the various West Indian jurisdictions and the archives of overseas bodies which have an interest in the West Indies, such as missionary societies. A programme called the Eastern Caribbean Documentation Project has been established to acquire such materials, under which a purchasing consortium has been formed consisting of the Main Library, the Faculty of Law Library and the Department of History of the UWI, Cave Hill; the Barbados Department of Archives; and the Barbados Public Library. The inclusion of the Department of History in this grouping, even to the extent of its providing funding, is of particular interest, given the discussions elsewhere in this volume on the degree of co-operation possible between libraries and teaching departments at universities. The funds contributed to the consortium are pooled and used chiefly to purchase microfilms from the Public Record Office of documents relating to the Eastern Caribbean, much of which is being filmed for the first time. Under the project, the Faculty of Law Library has succeeded in acquiring on microfilm virtually all pre-1900 legislation relating to the English-speaking islands. The project also has been fortunate to attract outside funding to assist with its purchasing, mainly from the University's Research and Publications Fund and from UNESCO.

Since collection development is in some measure a matter of resource allocation, it might be of interest at this stage to examine briefly the way in which available resources are allocated at Cave Hill. Those who would prefer to see a more detailed account of the process are referred to Michael E. Gill's paper on the subject.*

After funds have been set aside for journal subscriptions (about 40 percent of the total) and for the purchase of items for special collections and materials of an inter-disciplinary nature (about 20 percent of the remainder), the sum available in the book-vote is divided between the teaching departments in accord-ance with a formula which assigns to each course taught a value

---

*Michael E. Gill, "Parameters of Expenditure: The Allocation of Funds for the Purchase of Materials and Services to Support the Information Needs of the University Community in Science and Technology." Paper presented to the UNESCO/IFLA Exchange of Experience Seminar for Developing Countries, Deutsches Museum, Munich, 16-19 August 1983. University Libraries in Developing Countries: Structure and Function in Regard to Information Transfer for Science and Technology.

which is expressed in terms of "library units-of-account." The formula takes into consideration the following variables:

1. The weighting of the course (i.e., half course, full course, double course).
2. The number of students reading the course (the weighting ranges from 4, with less than 13 students on a course, to 8, with more than 100).
3. The degree to which the subject is reliant upon books (on a scale from 2, for laboratory subjects, to 5).
4. The average cost of books in the discipline, as given in published sources, with a weighting of from 3 to 9.

Postgraduate programmes are given the status of courses, with recognition being given to the special demands which such programmes make upon the library.

The unit-of-account value of each course is determined by multiplying together the weightings for the variables listed above, and the money available is divided by the sum total of the units-of-account carried by all courses in order to produce a monetary value for each unit-of-account. Departments are allocated funds in accordance with the number of units-of-account which their courses command.

I have already indicated some of the advantages which are available to us as a result of our being part of an institution which has a physical presence throughout the Caribbean. If problems of distance and communication could be overcome, there would of course be opportunities for even greater co-operation and resource sharing. Happily, certain technological advances, planned and in operation, should go some way toward easing these difficulties, and I will conclude by outlining these developments.

The libraries of UWI have for some time been examining the possibilities which exist for automation, and have in some cases begun to automate certain functions. While their distance from one another and the different circumstances which obtain at the three campuses limit the opportunities for the adoption of identical solutions at each campus, nevertheless we are seeking to maximise the extent to which automation will bring a greater degree of co-operation and interdependence among the libraries. The compilation of a union list of serials and the co-operative indexing of West Indian serial publications are two areas likely to be given priority in the automation plans for the three campuses. The use of OCLC by each campus for its current cataloguing, which is under serious consideration, would eventually give us access to each other's holdings and should produce a sharp increase in inter-library loan traffic within the university itself.

The second techological development to which I referred is one which, as the expansion of its acronym suggests, is not directly related to the university libraries, but it is one whose utility the libraries have been quick to recognise. The University is currently engaged in an experiment known as UWIDITE, the University of the West Indies Distance Teaching Experiment, which has as its prime aim the provision of teaching in the non-campus countries by means of a telecommunications link. At present, in addition to the main campus territories, only Dominica and St. Lucia are included in the network, but if the experiment were to prove successful and funding could be found, the intention would be to make reception possible in all non-campus countries.

The link that has been established for the purpose of the experiment, utilising satellite, microwave transmissions and land-line, is available 24 hours a day, and the libraries have been able to utilise some of the spare capacity on the circuit for the holding of administrative teleconferences, for staff-development seminars, and for the transaction of more mundane matters such as inter-library loans and the requesting of photo-copies. There is no doubt that since its funding in 1982 the UWIDITE link has brought the libraries significantly closer. If it becomes a permanent part of UWI life, we should see the campus libraries placing an ever-increasing reliance on each other's collections.

Specialized Research Collections:
Latin American Legal Resources

6. CURRENT LEGAL RESEARCH TRENDS IN LATIN AMERICA

Rubens Medina

The purpose of this paper is to present a broad overview of the subjects of current interest to researchers of Latin American law and to identify topics that are likely to become the focus of future research. Discussions of the specific needs and interests of particular organizations such as law firms, international business groups, and the courts are deliberately avoided. Instead, the paper focuses on the general concerns of academic institutions and government agencies, whose research interests tend to be the widest in scope.

How does one go about finding acceptable indicators for issues and trends in Latin American legal research? There are many ways to approach this question. Legislation, of course, is not only a primary source of law but, according to predominant contemporary theories, is also a reflection of the higher and more cherished values, a protector of the interests of society as well as an indication of future directions. Another acceptable indicator is the material being printed in law journals. More than books, the articles in journals reflect issues of current concern. They are the first line of intellectual response to legal issues and, therefore, trendsetters in this regard. Issues that are selected by local legal scholars are very likely to be those deserving the most attention and are, certainly, the most significant ones for the country or region in which they are written.

Because in civil law countries the written statutes and regulations are the ultimate synthesis of law as an instrument of justice and social control, one may then hypothesize that the more frequently a subject is legislated upon, the more likely these subjects are to elicit a similar frequency of response by legal practitioners and scholars. These responses, in turn, are likely to be reflected first in articles in legal periodicals and later in more comprehensive monographic works. Monographic works or treatises are more often than not the final evolutionary phase of subjects previously treated by journal authors.

Locating the first category of indicators, the legislation or laws themselves, is done in the Hispanic Law Division of the Library of Congress via the Index to Latin American Legislation,

---

Editor's Note. This paper was prepared from notes used by Dr. Medina for his address to SALALM XXIX.

a finding aid maintained by the Division which covers the region's legislative activities from 1950 to date. Included are about 30,000 entries a year from a total of twenty-two Spanish- and Portuguese-speaking countries. The second category, legal periodicals, may be found in the Hispanic Law Division through the Index to Latin American Legal Periodicals. This research instrument consists of records of 407 journal titles from Latin America, Spain, and Portugal, and contains approximately 4,600 entries per year.

With regard to the third category, books written on various legal subjects, a survey of the Law Library's records of monograph holdings over the last ten years indicates that the subject most frequently assigned to specific items was "Government Organization," with 3,742 items. Any inferences made from this figure might suggest, at least on paper, an increase in government organizational complexity and in its functions or services. A closer look at a random sample of items showed that the action most commonly undertaken was the establishment of new agencies. These new agencies were, of course, given new functions for the fulfillment of their mission. It is, therefore, expected that some of this growth will be reflected in administrative law, by adding new chapters, sections, or provisions, or by refining existing general principles into more specific, case-oriented, usable standards. This is clearly consistent with legal developments in other countries that have experienced the same evolutionary trends. It is no mystery that throughout most of the Western hemisphere governments have absorbed an increasing number of new functions: more control, more services, and so on. This should, therefore, be an area of special concern to everyone in the business of collecting and processing information.

Another subject found to be frequently indexed is "Commerce and Industry," with a total of 2,809 items computed for the last eight years. It is easy to speculate about the main components of this subject. A closer look into the items themselves reveals that approximately 30 percent of the material is related to international treaties and agreements concerning international trade and import-export, and about 30 percent of this category is related to incentives to either trade or industry. Another 20 percent is related to taxation and variations of it, and 10 percent to quality and price control, the latter containing also some items aimed at consumer protection. The remaining 10 percent consists of miscellaneous items such as restrictions on sales, reporting to government agencies, credit, and so on.

Other subjects frequently assigned are: "Zoning and Urban Development," 927 items; "Food and Drug," 886 items; "Education," 789; "Agriculture," 658; "Banks and Banking," 581. "Treaties and Agreements" should be considered a special category rather than a subject despite its high level of frequency. It is obviously a heading more reflective of a type of instrument, the subject of which varies greatly. Items in this category may also be found under specific subject headings such as "Commerce and Industry," "Technical Assistance," "Communication and Transportation," "Public Health," or "Copyright."

It is important to note here that some American legal scholars like Kenneth Karst of The University of California, Los Angeles, believe that there are marked background differences between legal research trends in the United States and those in Latin America. He sees the differences as follows:

A. A view of the role of law in the community that differs considerably from attitudes in the United States and Western Europe.

B. A degree of disparity between the written law and law in action that is characteristic of the world's developing societies.

C. A varying social structure that ranges from modern, highly westernized to the semifeudal.

D. A rate of social change whose rapidity seriously strains institutional frameworks.*

Further evidence of these differences, the same scholar notes, stems from Latin America's codified tradition, where research tends to follow a rather abstract approach compared with the very pragmatic--that is, concrete--problem-solving approach of the common law tradition (pp. 231-233). Professor John P. Goldbert of Southwestern University School of Law suggests the existence of still more differences which lie beyond the scope of this discussion.

The working hypothesis originally set forth in this paper should be qualified to include some of the elements related to the background differentials suggested by the American scholars cited. But the qualifiers should be related clearly and directly to the general political atmosphere that, in some nations of the region, indicates the predominance of oppressive government, a general state of violence and unrest, and other disrupting factors. These may doubtless reduce or eliminate the free flow of contributions from practitioners and scholars in the areas or subjects of concrete serious concern. Thus, although there may be some truth in the assessment of our American colleagues, we should be prepared to detect and recognize some of the more obvious current conditions preventing legal practitioners and scholars in Latin America from following practical approaches to meaningful issues.

---

*Kenneth L. Karst, Law and Development in Latin America: A Case Book (Los Angeles, CA: University of California Press, 1975).

Returning to the matter of sources, one finds that legal periodicals show the following subjects to be the most frequently studied: Constitutional Law, Civil Code, Civil Procedure, Criminal Code, Criminal Procedure, Corporations, Domestic Relations, Labor Law, International Law, and Taxation. All of these are clearly very broad in character. The same subjects and related frequency are reflected in the records of the monographic works.

Concerning new trends, the following subjects were found in all three source categories: Copyright, Space, Nuclear Energy, Consumer Protection, Women, Automation, Human Organ Transplants and New Special Medical/Surgical Procedures, and the Environment.

In conclusion, and as a general rule, legal research continues to rely on primary sources such as official gazettes and compilations of laws and regulations. Special attention must be paid, however, to capturing the legal literature covering the most frequently legislated subjects and the literature related to new subjects.

7.   LATIN AMERICAN LEGAL MATERIALS: REFERENCE AND BIBLIOGRAPHIC SOURCES

Selma Cervetti de Rodríguez

Latin American nations share with Europe a legal heritage that can be traced to Rome. They are countries of written law, in which the law derives from express enactment rather than from custom or tradition, and in which official publication is a condition of validity.

A serious study of any topic in the social sciences--particularly in the fields of economics, history, sociology, and political science--requires a review of the legal aspects of the problem. For instance, in order to appraise the impact of the 1973 oil crisis on Latin American countries, both existing petroleum laws and newly designed types of contracts for oil exploration must be examined. A similar procedure should be followed when studying the situation of women, foreign investments, and other issues in these countries.

The basic research routine suggested by Vaclav Mostecky, former International Law Librarian at Harvard Law School, in his article "Reference Service in Foreign Law" (55 L. Lib. J. 386 [1962]), may be followed effectively by anyone using Latin American legal materials. Mostecky summed up the process in seven steps:

1.   Consult an English language treatise on the subject.

2.   If the answer is not there, consult a foreign language treatise on the subject and follow its footnotes to laws and court decisions.

3.   Consult recent periodical articles and follow the same procedure.

4.   Search through the indexes to codes, or commentaries to codes, or indexes to legislation when available. For treaties, consult texts on public or private international law.

5.   For some countries, consult looseleaf services to legislation, digests, and repertoires, which refer both to laws and to court decisions. The annual reports of central banks and ministries such as Foreign Relations, Economics and Finance, or

Editor's Note. This paper was prepared from notes used by the author for her address to SALALM XXIX.

Education are useful in researching the law in Latin American countries.

6. When a pertinent section of the code or law is found, search through the most current issues of official gazettes for amendments or changes in the legislation.

7. Consult related treatises and compilations of laws of the country.

More than twenty years after the Mostecky article was published the research procedure is still valid, and only a few sources need be added. These include the work accomplished by international and regional organizations such as the Organization of American States, the Inter-American Development Bank, the United Nations Food and Agriculture Organization, the World Health Organization, the Asistencia Recíproca Petrolera Estatal Latinoamericana (ARPEL), and the Asociación Latinoamericano de Integración (ALADI).

Categories of Legal Materials

A very broad classification of Latin American legal materials includes three major categories:

Statutory

The actual texts of the laws and regulations, including treaties. The main source for statutory materials is the Diario oficial (Official Gazette) of each country, which is published by the Imprenta Nacional (National Printing Office) or by a body designated by the law to be the official government publisher. Collections of these statutory materials are usually published annually by the country's Imprenta Nacional. Commercial vendors in the United States, such as Oceana Publications and Matthew Bender, also produce collections of these statutes arranged by subject.

Doctrinal

Treatises, textbooks, and so on about specific topics of the law. A large body of material is available in the Spanish language, published mainly in Mexico, Chile, Argentina, and Uruguay.

Reference and Research Tools

a. General introductory materials about national and regional legal systems.--If the investigation is to be exhaustive, an excellent reading knowledge of Spanish is necessary. If, however, only general concepts are to be researched, one can find a considerable amount of literature written in English. The appended bibliography (s.v. "General") identifies several very good sources for understanding the basic Latin American legal

system.   Clear,   extensive   explanations   of   Roman   law,   the
Justinian Code, Spanish law, and other sources of Latin American
law can be found in these works, as can explanations of the
contemporary Inter-American legal system under what is today the
Organization of American States.

b. The publications of agencies other than the national
printing   offices.--These   include   (1) ministries;   (2) national
libraries (including the U.S. Library of Congress); (3) professional associations, such as the International Association of Law
Libraries,   the   American   Association   of   Law   Libraries,   the
American Society of International Law, and colegios de abogados;
(4) university   law   schools;   (5) regional   political   and   special
interest   organizations   such   as   the   Organization   of   American
States, ARPEL, the World Health Organization, ALADI, the
Asociación   Latinoamericana   de   Instituciones   Financieros   de
Desarrollo (ALIDE), the United Nations Economic Commission
for Latin America, and the Andean Group; and (6) research
institutes such as the Instituto para la Integración de América
Latina (INTAL).

c.   Dictionaries and encyclopedias.

Background Materials

The   first   requisite   in   researching   legal   materials   is   to
refer to a good encyclopedia: the Enciclopedia jurídica Omeba is
the most popular one and is consulted by practicing lawyers
throughout Latin America.   It is a twenty-six-volume work with
irregularly published supplements.

It is said that 35 percent of the Anglo-American legal
language is Latin.   In view of this, many questions can be
answered by consulting the two most popular law dictionaries
published in the United States: Black's Law Dictionary, published
by West, and Ballantine's Law Dictionary, published by Lawyers'
Co-op.

Other useful background sources that are readily available in
the United States include:

Martindale-Hubell Law Directory.   Published every year.
Volume 7 contains a section on foreign law arranged by
country.

International Encyclopedia of Comparative Law.   Volume 1
consists of separately published fascicles of national
reports of individual countries.

Statement of the Laws in Matters Affecting Business
In . . . .   A series published by the Organization of
American States.   Unfortunately, many of the volumes are
outdated.   The most recent treats Honduras, and at this
writing it is already two years old.   General information
is   given   by   subject   category   along   with   the   laws

applicable to it.   The reports are prepared by notable
lawyers from the countries covered.

Current Legislation

The sources named above give a general idea of how the
subject is treated in each country, along with, in some cases,
some of the laws applicable to it.   But one of the frequent
requests that law librarians receive is to provide information on
current legislation.   The Index to Latin American Legislation,
issued by the Library of Congress, is a basic research tool.   It
enables one to trace pertinent legislation on specific subjects
along with amendments to that legislation.   Another important
U.S. source for current information is Matthew Bender's series,
Doing Business in . . . , which thus far covers Mexico and
Brazil.   Because it is also important to determine which legislation
prevails over others in the different countries, Rubens Medina's
Nomenclature and Hierarchy: Basic Latin American Legal Sources
is also a useful source.

Legal Hierarchies

The most important of all laws in Latin America are the
constitutions of each country.   If a constitutional government is
overthrown in a coup d'etat, one of the first measures taken by
the new rulers is to announce either that the present constitution
remains or that, while a new one is being drafted, the country
will be ruled according to another specific instrument. Constitutions include the affirmation of principles of the State, the
rights of its citizens and inhabitants, and an outline of the
organization and administration of government.   Since the
Constitution is the supreme law of the land, in all cases of
conflict between the Constitution and another type of law, the
constitutional provision prevails.   It is the duty of the Supreme
Court to decide upon the status of all legal acts challenged for
constitutionality.

Usually there are many published editions of a constitution.
The official version prevails, of course.   Oceana Publishers,
Inc., one of the preeminent U.S. publishers of legal materials,
produces Constitutions of the Countries of the World, consisting
of twenty-four binders in looseleaf format.   Periodic installments
update the collection.

Codes, which are also adopted by legislative acts, are the
next most important instruments taken into consideration by
judges in reaching decisions.   The most important of these is the
Civil Code, which regulates the fundamental institutions of private
law.   Other codified subjects are the commercial, penal, judicial,
civil and penal procedure, labor, agrarian, mining, petroleum, and
water codes of each country.

A law comes into being when it is approved by the legisla-
ture.   Subsequently, the President or chief of state announces

that it is being promulgated. It becomes binding after it appears in the country's official gazette, generally after the third day of publication. In all cases, its binding force is stated in the last clause: "This law will be in force after three days, or starting in January of X year." All Latin American countries, except Paraguay, publish an official gazette on a regular basis.

Major Publishers of Legal Materials by Country

Argentina

The three major publishers of legal sources are Astrea/De Palma, Abeledo Perrot, and La Ley. The first publishes primarily doctrinal materials and textbooks. The second publishes annotated editions of the country's Constitution and codes. One of the most active and important professionals in this field is the Librarian of Judicial Power, Miguel Danielian. Dr. Danielian contributes annually to the new editions of the codes published by Abeledo Perrot by painstakingly keeping track of legislation as published daily in the Boletín oficial. La Ley publishes collections of statutes in the Anales de legislación and Repertorio, and other services, including Jurisprudencia de la Corte Suprema de Justicia de la Nación a través de la Constitución Nacional.

Bolivia

The Imprenta Nacional publishes La gaceta oficial but does not issue cumulative volumes. Most research activity is done instead at the private level. Legal books are published and distributed primarily by Amigos del Libro and by Werner Guttentag in Cochabamba.

Brazil

In addition to the Diario oficial, the compilation of laws most frequently used by lawyers is the Coletanea de lex nacional e provincial. Also widely used is Carteira Forense Konfino, a thick manual containing the Constitution and codes; a new edition is published by J. Konfino (Rio de Janeiro) every five or six years. The amount of legal literature is enormous. Susan Bach (Rua Martins Ferreira, 32, 22271 Rio de Janeiro) is the primary bookdealer for obtaining these publications.

Chile

In addition to the Diario oficial, the Controloría General de la República publishes the Recopilación de leyes in two volumes. The first contains decree laws, the second contains regulatory decrees. They are available from Editorial Jurídica de Chile, the country's major publisher of legal materials. The Biblioteca del Congreso is also very active. It records the status of legislation and struggles to computerize the millions of cards on file.

Research results are published in the Boletín de la Biblioteca del Congreso, which also includes bibliographies.

Colombia

The Diario oficial is not cumulated, and only recently has an index been published. Legislación Económica is a vendor that performs the same role as some legal publishers in the United States. They produce a great number of publications designed to be used by lawyers in their daily activities. Unfortunately, all are published in looseleaf format. The noted law schools at the Universities Javariana and del Rosario publish scholarly research resources, and Temis publishes law books.

Costa Rica

The lack of a detailed table of contents makes the Diario oficial difficult to use. The Imprenta Nacional publishes an annual compilation of the laws in a multivolume set.

Ecuador

The Registro Oficial produces an index of legislation every month, but no yearbook is published. The Cooperación de Estudios y Publicaciones frequently publishes updated individual laws during the year. An index to the legislation is published annually in the Indice de legislación ecuatoriana. As in Argentina, a Repertorio de legislación is produced. Published in two volumes, it covers the years 1830-1975, and should be used in conjunction with the yearly indexes. Unfortunately, there are no cumulative volumes yet.

Guatemala

The "Diario oficial" is the Diario de Centroamérica, which supersedes El Guatemalteco. Compilations have been issued, but the last volume was published in 1976-1977.

Haiti

Le Moniteur publishes no indexes or cumulative volumes. The laws and decrees are not numbered, which complicates research considerably. The Code, the Lois usuels, is designed to be a quick reference tool but does not cover all necessary subjects. Moreover, it is out of date.

Honduras

The very inconvenient format of the Diario oficial results in a bulky bound volume. There are no yearly compilations. But Leyes y códigos de Honduras is a two-volume publication that includes most important instruments: civil, commercial, procedural codes, and so forth.

Mexico

Since 1978 the Diario oficial has published a very convenient annual "Separata legislativa." Editorial Porrua is the major publisher of statutory materials as well as textbooks and doctrinal materials. Research is also done at universities such as the Universidad Iberoamericana, which publishes a good legal periodical, Jurídica. In addition, the Ministry of Foreign Relations has made available a collection of the treaties signed by Mexico from 1810 onward. Included is a one-volume index to the collection.

Nicaragua

An important source for recent information is the semi-annual Decreto-Leyes para gobierno de un país a través de una Junta de Gobierno de Reconstrucción Nacional, compiled and published since 1979 by Rolando D. Lacayo and Martha Lacayo de Arauz.

Panama

La gaceta oficial has no cumulative yearbook.

Paraguay

Paraguay is the only country in Latin America that does not publish a Diario oficial or its equivalent. To help fill this void, well-known lawyer Francisco Mersán, owner of Organización Labor, produces a Bolétin that contains all approved legislation as well as a tax calendar. A subscription costs around $330 a year. Mersán also publishes every two or three years a volume called Legislación fiscal, which has become a kind of Código fiscal, accepted and used daily by lawyers. The publisher, La Ley, plays an important part in Paraguay as well as in Argentina. For example, its publication, La ley; revista jurídica paraguaya, is one of the very few legal periodicals published regularly in that country. International instruments such as treaties and international agreements entered into by Paraguay are published by the Ministry of Foreign Relations.

Peru

El peruano; normas legales is a "separata" of El peruano and represents a major improvement in the publishing of statutory materials over the previous full format newspaper, which made research a true hardship. An index is provided monthly. The Colección legislativa, published by the Cámara de Diputados, is a compilation of the laws which is valuable because the laws are correlated. The Biblioteca del Congreso has also inaugurated a series of bibliographies; unfortunately, only one installment has been published as of this writing.

El Salvador

The Diario oficial is published daily, but no yearly compilation is available.

Uruguay

The Diario oficial issues cumulative volumes every year.

Venezuela

The Gaceta oficial publishes special issues covering important pieces of legislation. However, Ramírez y Garay publishes fortnightly the "Gaceta legal," which assembles all the important instruments that have appeared in the various issues of La gaceta oficial. The latter is the more convenient source to work with.

Regional Sources

Deserving of mention is the Institute for Latin American Integration (INTAL) in Buenos Aires, which published twenty-eight issues of a unique periodical, Derecho de la integración, in the 1960s. This is an excellent source for Researching Latin American integration during that period. In addition to articles about the legal aspects of integration, the journal regularly carried sections of statutory materials concerning the Andean Common Market, the former Latin American Free Trade Association (LAFTA), now Asociación Latinoamericana de Integración (ALADI), and decisions of national supreme courts which were connected with these regional organizations and the integration efforts. Unfortunately, Derecho de la integración, along with Revista de la integración and Boletín de información legal, also published by INTAL, were discontinued and were superseded by Integración latinoamericana.

SELECTED BIBLIOGRAPHY

Andean Group

Falconi R., Raul, ed. El Pacto Andino: texto y comentarios de los instrumentos constitutivos de las instituciones de la integración y de las decisiones y resoluciones de sus organismos. Quito: Andinas, 1973.

Garcia-Amador y Rodríguez, F. V. The Andean Legal Order: A New Community Law. Dobbs Ferry, NY: Oceana, 1978.

Junta del Acuerdo de Cartagena. Historia documental del Acuerdo de Cartagena. Buenos Aires: Instituto para la Integración de América Latina (INTAL), 1974.

_____. Ordenamiento jurídico del Acuerdo de Cartagena; instrumentos básicos, decisiones, resoluciones. 6 vols. Lima, 1982.

Collections of Statutes

"Constitutions of the Countries of the World." Dobbs Ferry, NY: Oceana, 19__.

International Centre for Settlement of Investments Disputes. "Investment Laws of the World." Dobbs Ferry, NY: Oceana, n.d. Looseleaf.

Olavarria Avila, Julio. Los códigos de comercio latinoamericanos con una introducción de derecho comparado externo. Santiago: Jurídico de Chile, 1961.

Organization of American States. Constitutions of Member States of the OAS. Dobbs Ferry, NY: Oceana, 1982.

_____. Mining and Petroleum Legislation: Latin America and the Caribbean. Dobbs Ferry, NY: Oceana, 1979.

Regimen de las inversiones extranjeras en los países de la ALALC; textos legales y procedimientos administrativos. Buenos Aires: INTAL, 197_.

Regimen de la transferencia de tecnología en los países de América latina; textos legales y procedimientos adminstrativos. Buenos Aires: INTAL, 197_.

Zabala, Juan Ovidio. Las constituciones vigentes. Buenos Aires: Perrot, 1961.

Constitutional

Demicheli, Alberto. Formación constitucional rioplatense. Montevideo: Barreiro y Ramos, 1956.

Gómez de la Torre, Mario A. Derecho constitucional interamericano. Quito: Universitaria, 1964.

Country Guides

Manigat, Leslie F., ed. The Caribbean Yearbook of International Relations. Leiden: A. W. Sijthoff, 19__.

A Statement of the Laws of . . . in Matters Affecting Business. Washington, DC: OAS, 19__.

Dictionaries

Argeri, Saul A. Diccionario de derecho comercial y de la empresa. Buenos Aires: Astrea, 1982.

Anderson, William S., ed. Ballantine's Law Dictionary with Pronunciations. 3d ed. Rochester, NY: Lawyer's Co-op, 1969.

Baleyte, Jean, et al. Dictionnaire juridique: français-anglais, English-French. Paris: Navarre, 1977.

Barraine, Raymond. Nouveau dictionnaire de droit et de sciences economiques. 4th ed. Paris: Librairie Generale.

Black, Henry Campbell. Black's Law Dictionary. Rev. 4th ed. St. Paul, MN: West, 1968.

Casso y Romero, Ignacio de, and Francisco Cervera. Diccionario de derecho privado: derecho civil, común y foral; derecho mercantil; derecho notarial y registral; derecho canónico. México, DF: Labor, 1961.

Codera Martín, José Maria. Diccionario de derecho mercantil. Madrid: Pirámide, 1979.

Corniot, S. Dictionnaire de droit. Paris: Dalloz, 1966.

Couture, Eduardo J. Vocabulario jurídico, con especial referencia al derecho procesal positivo vigente uruguayo. Montevideo: Facultad de Derecho, 1960.

Dietl, Clara Erika. Dictionary of Legal, Commercial and Political Terms with Illustrative Examples, Explanatory Notes and Commentaries on Comparative Law. English–German, Englisch–Deutsch. New York, NY: Matthew Bender, 1979.

Fernández Vázquez, Emilio. Diccionario de derecho público; administrativo, constitucional, fiscal. Buenos Aires, 1981.

Ferreira, Aurelio Buarque de Hollanda. Pequeño dicionário brasileiro da língua portuguesa. 11th ed. Rio de Janeiro: Civilização Brasileira, 1967.

Goldstein, Raul. Diccionario de derecho penal y criminología. 2d ed. Buenos Aires: Astrea.

Guillien, Raymond, and Jean Vincent. Lexique de termes juridiques. 12th ed. Paris: Dalloz, 1972.

Herbst, Robert. Dictionary of Commerce, Finance and Law. Zug: Translegal, 1976.

Hwevar, Robert. Dictionary of Commercial, Financial and Legal Terms. Zug: Translegal, 1979.

Jordana de Pozas, Luis. Dictionnaire juridique: français-espagnol, espagnol-français. Paris: Navarre, 1968.

Moreno Rodríguez, Rogelio. Vocabulario de derecho y ciencias sociales. Buenos Aires: Ediciones Depalma, 1974.

Nunes, Pedro dos Reis. Dicionário de tecnología jurídica. 11th ed. Rio de Janeiro: Livraría Freitas Bastos, 1982.

Orgaz, Arturo. Diccionario de derecho y ciencias sociales. Cordoba: Assandri, 1961.

Paenson, Isaac. Manual of the Terminology of Public International Law (Law of Peace) and International Organizations: English-French-Spanish-Russian. Brussels: E. Bruylant, 1983.

Pérez Caballero, Aurelio. Diccionario jurídico peruano. Lima: Juan Mejía Baca, 1972.

Pina Vara, Rafael de. Diccionario de derecho. 10th ed. México, DF: Porrúa, 1981.

Quemner, Thomas A. Dictionnaire juridique: français-anglais. Paris: Navarre, 1969.

Ramirez Gronda, Juan D. Diccionario jurídico. 6th ed. Buenos Aires: Claridad, 1965.

Robb, Louis A. Dictionary of Legal Terms: Spanish-English and English-Spanish. New York, NY: John Wiley & Sons, 1955.

Silva, De Plácido. Vocabulario jurídico. 7th ed. Río de Janeiro: Forense, 1982.

Vitral, Waldir. Vocabulario jurídico: volume v, A-Z. 2d ed. Río de Janeiro: Forense, 1982.

The World Bank Glossary: English, French, Spanish. Washington, DC: World Bank, 1981.

Encyclopedias

Cabanellas, Guillermo. Diccionario de derecho usual. Buenos Aires: Atalaya (1946).

Enciclopedia jurídica Omeba. 26 vols. and appendixes. Buenos Aires: Bibliográfica Argentina, 19__.

International Encyclopedia of Comparative Law. The Hague: Martinus Nijhoff, 19__.

General

De Vries, Henry P., and José Rodríguez-Novas. The Law of the Americas: An Introduction to the Legal Systems of the American Republics. Dobbs Ferry, NY: Oceana, 1965.

Golbert, Albert S., and Yenny Nun. Latin American Laws and Institutions. New York, NY: Praeger, 1982.

González, Armando E. "The Role of Latin American Legal Material in the Social Science Research Library." Law Library Journal, 52 (1971), 64.

Karst, Kenneth L., and Keith S. Rosenn. Law and Development in Latin America. Berkeley, CA: University of California Press, 1975.

Karst, Kenneth L., and Jane R. Trapnell. Latin American Legal Institutions: Problems for Comparative Study. Berkeley, CA: University of California Press, 1966.

Reference

Kleckner, Simone-Marie, and Blanka Kudej. International Legal Bibliography. Dobbs Ferry, NY: Oceana, 1983.

Medina, Rubens, and Cecilia Medina Quiroga. Nomenclature and Hierarchy: Basic Latin American Legal Sources. Washington, DC: Library of Congress, 1979.

Wallach, Kate, ed., for Committee on Foreign and International Law of American Association of Law Libraries. Union List of Basic Latin American Legal Materials. South Hackensack, NJ: Fred B. Rothman, 1971.

Social Security

La seguridad social en los países del Grupo Andino: documentos ocasionales; estudio comparativo (versión provisional). Washington, DC: Organicación de Estados Americanos, Programa de Desarrollo Social, 1979.

Treaties

García-Amador y Rodríguez, comp. Sistema interamericano a través de tratados, convenciones y otros documentos. Washington, DC: Organización de Estados Americanos, 1981.

Inter-American Institute of International Legal Studies. Instruments of Economic Integration in Latin America and in the Caribbean. Dobbs Ferry, NY: Oceana, 1975.

Lawson, Ruch. International Regional Organizations: Constitutional Foundations. New York, NY: Praeger, 1962.

8. LEGAL MATERIALS FROM LATIN AMERICA AND THE CARIBBEAN: SOME IDEAS FOR ACQUISITION

Ellen G. Schaffer

The proceedings of the fifteenth Seminar on the Acquisition of Latin American Library Materials, held at the University of Toronto, June 23-26, 1970, include a number of papers addressing issues relevant to the acquisition of Latin American legal resources.[1] Fourteen years later I would like to be able to report that many of the difficulties described therein have changed sufficiently to allow for the development of orderly selection and acquisition processes. Unfortunately, this is not generally the case. At the 1970 Seminar, Fernando J. Figueredo quoted a Spanish proverb: "suerte te dé Dios, que el saber te vale poco," or in English, "Ask God for luck, since knowledge will be of little help to you."[2] I suggest that good fortune combined with language knowledge, a familiarity with the legal systems involved, a tenacity of spirit, and a sense of humor are all requisites to the successful pursuit of Latin American and Caribbean legal materials. Since the proceedings of SALALM XV are published and available for consultation, I will not repeat all the problems outlined there. Instead, I offer here what I hope are some creative, unusual methods of identifying and locating copies of legal publications.

If one provides reference service and also has responsibility for the acquisition of Latin American and Caribbean legal collections, then reference requests will often help structure the type of resources needed. Very often, when faced with a reference question concerning an unfamiliar area, the best plan is to first consult resources such as the Statement of the Laws of the OAS Member States in Matters Affecting Business,[3] updated at infrequent intervals by the Organization of American States, or the section "Digest of the Laws of Other Countries" in the Martindale-Hubbell Law Directory.[4]

The series of guides to foreign legal systems published by the Library of Congress includes many on Latin American nations. Most were published in the 1940s but still serve as valuable sources of information. Two of the guides that have been revised in recent years are A Revised Guide to the Law and Legal Literature of Mexico by Helen L. Clagett and David M. Valderrama[5] published in 1973 and Law and Legal Literature of Peru by David M. Valderrama[6] published in 1976.

James E. Herget and Jorge Camil are authors of An Introduction to the Mexican Legal System[7] published in 1978. In addition to offering a historical overview, this work includes sections on different aspects of the law, for example, constitutions, civil law, property and succession, business and investment, and criminal law. Included are sample documents, an English-language bibliography organized by subject, and a glossary of Mexican legal terms. Another title that furnishes a historical review of legal developments in Latin America as well as a discussion of the internal legal aspects particular to the region is Latin American Laws and Institutions by Albert S. Goldbert and Yenny Nun.[8]

In 1977, the American Association of Law Libraries published Basic Latin American Legal Materials, 1970-1975 by Juan F. Aguilar and Armando E. González.[9] Divided by country, it includes bibliographic entries for constitutions, major codes, laws organized by subject, and law-related monographs.

A variety of sources of information and publishers can be identified from my 1977 Guide to Latin American Business Information Sources[10] and its sequel, Business Information Sources of Latin America and the Caribbean.[11] For an informative overview of Latin American legal systems and how they relate to social science research collections, see "The Role of Latin American Legal Material in the Social Science Research Library" by Armando E. González.[12]

Once the types of publications to be acquired are known, the tasks of locating and selecting titles and, of course, acquiring them, follow. Both Libros en venta en Hispanoamérica y España[13] and Fichero bibliográfico hispanoamericano[14] include titles under the subject division "Derecho"; however, to select a title from either of these publications and attempt to order it from the publisher is not likely to be successful. In Latin America, the number of copies printed for any given title is invariably much smaller than in the United States. Moreover, while the "current" codes (civil, criminal, commercial, civil procedure, and criminal procedure) for those Latin American countries whose legal publishing industry is larger and more organized might be listed in either Libros en venta or Fichero, for many countries no titles appear.

To order the titles found, regular order forms (and/or slips) should be used only if they are bilingual. The chances of success increase dramatically if each order or batch of orders is accompanied by a personal letter in Spanish--or Portuguese or French, as the case may be. A bookstore that is also a publisher, such as Porrua in Mexico, will sell a broader scope of material than will a single publishing house. Also, depending upon the size of the bookstore/publisher, they may actually respond to inquiries with information that publications are out of print, temporarily out of stock, or available.

If an item is available, a "pro forma" invoice will most likely be sent, often to be paid in the nation's currency. Once

the publications are shipped, one must be prepared to wait--
occasionally a new edition may even come out before the order is
received (air mail delivery at additional cost may be requested by
so indicating in the original order or letter). For unavailable
titles and those that cannot be located in bibliographic lists, a
few alternative suggestions follow. Overall, it is important to be
imaginative and persistent; success in this acquisition process
takes time and effort.

Although everyone has had difficulties with ordering and
receiving materials from overseas, let me point out three personal
experiences that were positive. The first was with the Downtown
Book Center in Miami, Florida.[15] Its owner, José Rabadé, was an
invaluable asset to me when I was a purchaser for the Latin
American collection at the University of Miami's Law Library.
Although it often took a few months, Mr. Rabadé not only successfully acquired legal titles from many Latin American countries
but also provided a discount. If, for example, in looking for a
commercial code from Venezuela, I had not been able to identify a
particular edition, all I needed to specify was the title and
particular date. He would then locate a copy. All books were
shipped to the Downtown Book Center and then to the Law
Library along with a copy of our order with purchase numbers.
Payment to the Downtown Book Center was in dollars, a blessing
not to be taken lightly compared with asking a university's
Accounts Payable Office to pay an invoice in a foreign currency.

The Librería Adolfo Linardi y Risso[16] in Montevideo,
Uruguay, and Juan I. Risso, in particular, proved to be not only
reliable and professional but instructive as well. When first
contacted as to the availability of current codes for Uruguay,
Mr. Risso was kind enough to respond with a brief explanation of
that country's form of official legal publishing and offered to
supply our library with annotated editions of the codes from only
the more serious jurists.

Other publishers have also taken the time to respond to
acquisition requests or inquiries with more than just an abbre-
viated reply. The Faculty of Law at the University of the West
Indies has invariably provided me with helpful suggestions,
names, and addresses for further contacts in the Caribbean, and
even photocopies when necessary. They have answered a stream
of questions concerning the acquisition of Caribbean legal materials, and their staff was kind enough to send me a compilation of
the latest revised edition of laws of the Commonwealth Caribbean
territories arranged by jurisdiction. The 1979 publication, Legal
Literature and Publishing in the Commonwealth Caribbean: A
Working Paper,[17] by Velma Newton of the Faculty of Law Library
at the University of West Indies, contains an excellent description
of historical as well as current legal publishing in the Commonwealth Caribbean. The University of the West Indies Faculty of
Law Library also indexes the legislation of territories of the

West Indies under the West Indian Legislative Indexing Project
(WILIP),[18] providing an indispensable reference tool for researching the statutes and subsidiary legislation of these countries.

The publication Third World Bookdealers: A Selected List of
Bookdealers in Africa, Asia, and Latin America,[19] compiled by
Jennifer V. Magnus and Sylvia Csiffary, offers an extensive
listing of possible dealers, publishers, and others. SALALM has
recently published a Directory of Vendors of Latin American
Library Materials compiled by David Block and Howard L. Karno
which includes information on such matters as dealers; geographic
scope, availability of catalogs, type of stock, service, and
hours.[20] Many of the publishers and/or dealers listed in the
sources mentioned have mailing lists or catalogs that they will
gladly supply.

Often one learns of a new publication from a reader doing
research in a particular area of Latin American law, or, as
happened recently, through a newspaper article. The Washington
Post on April 22, 1984, discussed the issue of press freedom in
Nicaragua and referred to an emergency decree in effect since
1982. The pertinent legislation was found in the series of
Nicaraguan decrees, Decretos-leyes para gobierno de un país a
través de una Junta de Gobierno de Reconstrucción Nacional
received from Rolando D. Lacayo in Managua. If the law in
question had not yet been included, or if I had not been successful in locating it elsewhere, I would have written to Mr. Lacayo
for assistance.[21] I now make it a habit to read newspapers and
newsletters for announcements of new legal developments, and to
acquire copies of the items before a reader asks for them. It is
a way to develop and maintain contacts with people when not
under pressure to supply information.

Professors teaching or conducting research in Latin American
law can be tapped as resources for information and legislation as
they are frequently in contact with local counsel and/or law
professors in Latin America. For example, while at the University of Miami, I started a collection of Latin American legal
memoranda supplied by members of the local bar association.
These memoranda, always on topics of current legislative interest,
often included the text of new legislation.

It is also possible, of course, to contact the Hispanic Law
Division of the Library of Congress to request assistance in
identifying citations. The Hispanic Law Division regularly
indexes current Latin American legislation and publishes it in
five-year cumulations of the Index to Latin American Legislation.[22] Information covering current legislation from Latin
American official gazettes is also available at the Hispanic Law
Division at the Library of Congress: microfilm copies of Latin
American official gazettes can be ordered from the Library of
Congress Photoduplication Service in Washington, DC, on a
standing order basis by establishing a deposit account. In 1978

the International Journal of Law Libraries published my article, "A Selective Guide to Law Related Publications of Latin America and the Caribbean,"[23] which includes a list of the official gazettes of Latin America and the Caribbean.

Occasionally a law is reprinted in a variety of other sources, sometimes in English. For example, the Texas International Law Journal recently published a special Centennial issue covering "Law in Latin America,"[24] which includes "A Bibliography of Latin American Law: Primary and Secondary Sources in English." Charles Szladits's A Bibliography on Foreign and Comparative Law and its updates (in the Winter 1984 issue of the American Journal of Comparative Law) and annual supplements have sections on the "Translation of codes, acts and decrees."[25] The American Series of Foreign Penal Codes produced by the Criminal Law Education and Research Center of the New York University School of Law includes translations of criminal codes from many nations. At this writing I am aware of translations of both the Argentine and Colombian penal codes.[26] Oceana issues a series of looseleaf volumes on commercial, business, and trade laws of many of the world's nations containing "elusive" legislative texts in English.[27] The International Labour Office publishes a biennial Legislative Series that furnishes English translations of labor legislation from all parts of the world.[28] The Foreign Tax Law Association in Alachua, Florida, offers its members English-language looseleaf services on the tax and commercial laws of more than a hundred countries.[29] The service is expensive, but it is also updated frequently. The International Bureau of Fiscal Documentation publishes a Bulletin for International Fiscal Documentation that includes documentation and articles helpful for identifying review and tax legislation. A recent article, "Guatemala: An Overview of the 1983 Tax Reform," identifies the decree-laws that are currently in effect in that country.[30] The Bulletin of Legal Developments: A Fortnightly Survey of U.K., European, Foreign, Commonwealth and International Legal Affairs, published by the British Institute of International and Comparative Law, lists notices of new legislation from many countries and international organizations from around the world, including Latin America. Even though this service, which cites the first publication to mention the new legislation, does not give the location of the actual text of the law, it is an extremely current and useful method of disseminating the existence of new laws.[31] Serving a similar purpose are newsletters such as Business Latin America,[32] published weekly by Business International Corporation, and those published by Latin American Newsletters, Ltd.[33]

The monthly publication, Integración Latinoamericana, is an excellent source for documents from regional organizations and for identifying new developments in Latin American economic integration.[34] Organizations such as the Andean Group also publish monthly newsletters. Their Grupo Andino: carta informativa de la

Junta del Acuerdo de Cartagena prints the text of some of the new decisions by the group (in Spanish).[35] These documents are difficult to locate, so it may be worthwhile to subscribe to this publication. It may take months and several letters for the subscription to begin, as mine did, but I imagine it will now only cease when the publication itself does!

Specialized looseleaf services such as Mining and Petroleum Legislation of Latin America and the Caribbean[36] or Corporate Taxation in Latin America[37] provide useful, though often costly, methods of identifying legislation on particular subjects. The latter also has a listing of law offices with their addresses throughout Latin America which assist in the preparation of the service.

Central banks, government ministries, law schools, and other university libraries are also sources for publications for exchange or just for assistance. The results will, predictably, be varied. In searching for energy legislation, for example, I would first contact the library of an international corporation, such as an oil company. After searching in vain for a copy of the commercial code of Panama I wrote finally to the Director of the Legal Office of the Ministry of Commerce and Industry in Panama. The Director responded that the publication was 910 pages long and so could not be photocopied, but that a certain bookstore in Panama City had one remaining copy. I contacted the bookstore and within weeks had purchased and received a copy of the code.

The April 1983 Bulletin of the Florida Chapter of the Special Libraries Association has reprinted the papers from an SLA Florida Chapter Workshop on International Documents and Statistics. They include Salvador Miranda's "Dos and Don'ts When Acquiring Documents from Latin America and the Caribbean" along with three useful, even though not purely legal, lists provided by Mr. Miranda: a Directory of Latin American and Caribbean Approval Plan Book Dealers, a Directory of Latin American and Caribbean Statistical Agencies, and a Directory of Latin American and Caribbean National Central Banks.[38] I wish to thank Mr. Miranda, who is Latin American Bibliographer for the University of Florida Libraries, Gainesville, for allowing me to include his directories as appendixes to this paper. He asks that readers be aware that the entries were correct as of January, 1983; and, although he is unaware of any address changes, it is possible that some have occurred.

This paper has attempted to stress that although the acquisition of legal information from Latin America is very often a frustrating experience, it can be likened to a treasure hunt, and can result in success. Personal contacts, which can be made through correspondence if travel is not possible, is absolutely indispensable. Write lots of letters and make lots of contacts. Buena suerte!

Appendix A

Directory of Latin American and Caribbean Approval Plan Bookdealers

Mario Argueta
Barrio Abajo, 8a, Calle 210
Tegucigalpa, HONDURAS

Susan Bach
Rua Martins Ferreira, 32
2271 Rio de Janeiro, BRAZIL

Herta Berenguer L.
Correo 9, Casilla 16598
Santiage, CHILE

Caribbean Imprint Library
  Services
Box 350
West Falmouth, MA 92574 U.S.A.

Ricardo Rolon
Librería Comuneros
Casilla Correo 930
Asunción, PARAGUAY

Econolibros, S.A.
Apartado de Correos 38
Santo Domingo,
  DOMINICAN REPUBLIC

Fernando García Cambeiro
Cochabamba 244
(1150) Buenos Aires,
  ARGENTINA

Alfredo Montalvo
Editorial Inca
Apartado 1514
Cochabamba, BOLIVIA

Roso Helena Bahiana
I.N.E.D.
Rua Mexico, 31 s/1701
ZC-39 Rio de Janeiro, BRAZIL

E. Iturriaga y Cia.
Casilla 4640
Lima, PERU

Maurilia Mendoza de Jiménez
Casilla 430-A
Quito, ECUADOR

J. Noé Herrera
Libros de Colombia
Apartado Aereo 12053
Bogotá, COLOMBIA

Librería Hispanoamericana
Apartado 20830
Río Piedras, PUERTO RICO 00929

Juan I. Risso
Librería Adolfo Linardi
Juan Carlos Gómez 1435
Montevideo, URUGUAY

M.A.C.H.
P.O. Box 13-319
Delegación Benito Juárez
03500 México, DF, MEXICO

Sangster's Book Stores, Ltd.
P.O. Box 366
Kingston, JAMAICA

Librería Universal
P.O. Box 45035
(Shenandoah Station)
Miami, FL 33145 U.S.A.

Servicio de Difusión del Libro
Apartado Postal 185
San Salvador, EL SALVADOR

Soberbia, C.A.
Edificio Dillon, Local 4
Este 2, No. 139
Puenta Yanes a Tracabordo
Caracas 1010, VENEZUELA

Stephens & Johnsons, Ltd.
Books Department
P.O. Box 497
Port of Spain, TRINIDAD

Appendix B

Directory of Latin American and Caribbean Statistical Agencies

Statistics Division
Ministry of Finance
Redcliffe Street
St. John's, ANTIGUA

Instituto Nacional de
  Estadística y Censos
Hipólito Irigoyen 250, piso 12º.
Buenos Aires, ARGENTINA

Department of Statistics
P.O. Box N 3904
Nassau, BAHAMAS

Barbados Statistical Service
National Insurance Building
Fairchild Street
Bridgetown, BARBADOS

Central Planning Unit
Ministry of Finance and
  Economic Planning
Belmopan, BELIZE

Statistical Department
Ministry of Finance
Government Administration Bldg.
Hamilton, BERMUDA

Instituto Nacional de Estadística
Av. 6 de Agosto No. 2507
La Paz, BOLIVIA

Instituto Brasileiro de
  Geografia e Estadística (IBGE)
Directoria de Divulgação
Av. Brasil, 15 671-Lucas
21 241 Rio de Janeiro, BRAZIL

Planning Unit
Statistics Division
Road Town, Tortola,
  BRITISH VIRGIN ISLANDS

Instituto Nacional de Estadísticas
Casilla 7597, Correo 3
Santiago, CHILE

Departamento Administrativo
  Nacional de Estadística (DANE)
Apartado Aereo 80043
Bogotá, COLOMBIA

Dirección General de
  Estadística y Censos
Apartado 10163
San José, COSTA RICA

Comité Estatal de Estadística
Gaveta Postal 6016
La Habana, CUBA

Statistical Division
Ministry of Finance
22 Bath Road
Roseau, DOMINICA

Oficina Nacional de Estadística
Apartado de Correo 1342
Santo Domingo,
  DOMINICAN REPUBLIC

Instituto Nacional de
  Estadística y Censos
Av. 10 de Agosto 229
Quito, ECUADOR

Dirección General de
  Estadística y Censos
Calle Arce No. 953
San Salvador, EL SALVADOR

Central Statistics Office
Church Street
St. George's, GRENADA

Institut National de la Statis-
tique et des Etudes Economiques
Service Departamental de la
Guadeloupe
B.P. 96
Basseterre, GUADELOUPE

Dirección General de Estadística
40. Nivel
Edificio América
8a. Calle 9-55, Zona 1
Guatemala, GUATEMALA

Statistical Bureau
Ministry of Economic Development
Ministerial Building
P.O. Box 542
Georgetown, GUYANA

Institut National de Statistique
et des Etudes Economiques
Service Departamental de
la Guyane
B.P. 757
Cayenne, GUYANE

Institut Haïtien de Statistique
Boulevard Harry Truman
Cité de l'Exposition
Port-au-Prince, HAITI

Dirección General de
Estadística y Censos
6a. Av. y 8a. Calle, Comayaguela
Tegucigalpa, HONDURAS

Department of Statistics
9 Swallowfield Road
Kingston 5, JAMAICA

Institut National de la Statis-
tique et des Etudes Economiques
Service Departamental de la
Martinique
B.P. 605
Fort-de-France, MARTINIQUE

Coordinación General de los
Servicios Nacionales de
Estadística, Informática y
Geografía
Centeno No. 670
Colonia Granjas México
Delegación Inztacalco
08400 México, DF, MEXICO

Statistics Office
Government Headquarters
P.O. Box 292
Plymouth, MONTSERRAT

Instituto Nacional de
Estadística y Censos
Apartado 4031
Managua, NICARAGUA

Dirección de Estadística y Censos
Controloría General de la República
Apartado 5213
Panamá 5, PANAMA

Dirección General de Estadística
y Censos
Casilla Correo No. 1118
Asunción, PARAGUAY

Instituto Nacional de Estadística
Av. 28 de Julio No. 1056
Lima, PERU

Junta de Planificación
Apartado 41119
San Juan, PUERTO RICO

The Planning Unit
P.O. Box 186
Basseterre, ST. KITTS
(Also for NEVIS)

Statistical Department
Ministry of Development,
Planning and Statistics
Post Office Building
Castries, ST. LUCIA

The Statistical Unit
Kingston, ST. VINCENT

Algemeen Bureau voor
  de Statistiek
P.O. Box 244
Paramaribo, SURINAME

Central Statistical Office
P.O. Box 98
Port of Spain, TRINIDAD

Dirección General de
  Estadística y Censos
Secretaría de Planeamiento,
  Coordinación y Difusión
Cuareim 2052
Montevideo, URUGUAY

Oficina de Estadística
  e Informática
Apartado de Correos 4593
San Martín
Caracas, VENEZUELA

Appendix C

Directory of Latin American and Caribbean National/Central Banks

Banco de la Nación Argentina
Casilla de Correo 1294
Buenos Aires, ARGENTINA

Central Bank of the Bahamas
P.O. Box N 4868
Nassau, BAHAMAS

The Central Bank of Barbados
P.O. Box 1016
Treasury Building
Bridgetown, BARBADOS

The Government Savings Bank
The Treasury
Belize City, BELIZE

The Bank of Bermuda Ltd.
Front Street
Hamilton, 5-31, BERMUDA

Banco Central de Bolivia
Apartado Aereo 5947
La Paz, BOLIVIA

Banco de Brasil
Caixa Postal Aerea 562
Brasilia, BRAZIL

Virgin Islands National Bank
Road Town, Tortola,
 BRITISH VIRGIN ISLANDS

Government Savings Bank
George Town, Grand Cayman,
 CAYMAN ISLANDS

Banco Central de Chile
Sección Biblioteca
Casilla 967
Santiago, CHILE

Banco de la República
Carrera 7a., no. 14-78
Bogotá, COLOMBIA

Banco Central de Costa Rica
Apartado 2033
San José, COSTA RICA

Banco Nacional de Cuba
Calle Cuba no. 402
La Habana, CUBA

Bank Van de Nederlandse Antillen
Breedestraat 1 (P)
Willemstad, CURAÇAO

Banco Central de la
 República Dominicana
Calle Pedro Henríquez Ureña
Santo Domingo, DOMINICAN
 REPUBLIC

Banco Central del Ecuador
Casilla 339
Quito, ECUADOR

Banco Central de Reserva de
 El Salvador
1a. Calle Poniente 425
San Salvador, EL SALVADOR

Banques des Antilles Françaises
Place de la Victoire
Pointe-a-Pitre, GUADALOUPE

Banco de Guatemala
7a. Avenida 22-01
Zona 1
Guatemala, GUATEMALA

Banque de la Guyane
2, place Victor Schoelcher
Cayenne, GUYANE

Banque de la République d'Haïti
B.P. 1750
Port-au-Prince, HAITI

Banco Central de Honduras
P.O. Box C58
Tegucigalpa, HONDURAS

Bank of Jamaica
P.O. Box 621
Kingston, JAMAICA

Banque des Antilles Françaises
24-28 rue Lamartine
Fort-de-France, MARTINIQUE

Banco de México
Apartado Postal 98 - Bis.
México 1, DF, MEXICO

Banco Central de Nicaragua
Apartado 2252
Managua, NICARAGUA

Banco Nacional de Panamá
Apartado 5220
Panamá 5, PANAMA

Banco Central del Paraguay
Apartado Postal 861
Asunción, PARAGUAY

Banco de la Nación
Apartado Aereo 1835
Lima, PERU

Government Development Bank
  for Puerto Rico
P.O. Box 42001
San Juan, PUERTO RICO   00940

St. Kitts-Nevis National Bank Ltd.
P.O. Box 343
Basseterre, ST. KITTS

The National Commercial Bank
  of St. Vincent
P.O. Box 880
Kingston, ST. VINCENT

Centrale Bank van Suriname
P.O. Box 1801
Paramaribo, SURINAME

The Central Bank of Trinidad
  and Tobago
P.O. Box 1250
Port of Spain, TRINIDAD

Government Savings Bank
Grand Turk
TURKS AND CAICOS ISLANDS

Banco Central del Uruguay
Casilla de Correo 1467
Montevideo, URUGUAY

Banco Central de Venezuela
Apartado 2017
Caracas, 1010   VENEZUELA

NOTES

[1]Seminar on the Acquisition of Latin American Library Materials, XXV, Toronto, 1970, Final Report and Working Papers (Washington, DC: Organization of American States, 1971).

[2]Fernando J. Figueredo, "Acquisition of Latin American Legal Materials: A Burdensome Task," Law Library Journal, 64 (1971), 46-51.

[3]Statements of the Laws of the OAS Member States in Matters Affecting Business (Washington, DC: Organization of American States).

[4]Martindale-Hubbell Law Directory (Summit, NJ: Martindale-Hubbell, 1983).

[5]Helen L. Clagett and David M. Valderrama, A Revised Guide to the Law and Legal Literature of Mexico (Washington, DC: Library of Congress, 1973).

[6]David M. Valderrama, Law and Legal Literature of Peru (Washington, DC: Library of Congress, 1976).

[7]James E. Herget and Jorge Camil, An Introduction to the Mexican Legal System (Buffalo, NY: William S. Hein & Co., 1978).

[8]Albert S. Golbert and Yenny Nun, Latin American Laws and Institutions (New York, NY: Praeger, 1982).

[9]Juan F. Aguilar and Armando E. González, Basic Latin American Legal Materials, 1970-1975 (South Hackensack, NJ: Fred B. Rothman & Co., 1977). Published for the American Association of Law Libraries.

[10]Ellen G. Schaffer, Guide to Latin American Business Information Sources (Washington, DC: Organization of American States, 1977).

[11]Idem, Business Information Sources of Latin America and the Caribbean (Washington, DC: Organization of American States, 1982).

[12]Armando E. González, "The Role of Latin American Legal Material in the Social Science Research Library," Law Library Journal, 64 (1971), 52-64.

[13]Libros en venta en Hispanoamérica y España (San Juan, PR: Melcher Ediciones). Contact Melcher Ediciones, Apartado 6000, San Juan, PR 00906.

[14]Fichero bibliográfico hispanoamericano (San Juan, PR: Melcher Ediciones). See n. 13 for publisher's address.

[15]Downtown Book Center, 245 SE First Street, Suites 236-237, Miami, FL 33131. Phone (305) 377-9941.

[16]Librería Adolfo Linardi y Risso, Juan Carlos Gómez #1435, Montevideo, Uruguay.

[17]Velma Newton, Legal Literature and Publishing in the Commonwealth Caribbean: A Working Paper (Cave Hill, Barbados: Faculty of Law, University of the West Indies, 1979). Distributed by Wm. W. Gaunt & Sons, Inc., Homes Beach, FL.

[18]West Indian Legislative Indexing Project, University of the West Indies, Faculty of Law Library, P.O. Box 64, Bridgetown, Barbados. Also available from W. W. Gaunt & Sons, Inc., Homes Beach, FL.

[19]Jennifer Magnus and Sylvia Csiffary, Third World Book-dealers: A Selected List of Bookdealers in Africa, Asia, and Latin America (Chicago, IL: Resources & Technical Services Division, American Library Association, 1979).

[20]David Block and Howard L. Karno, A Directory of Vendors of Latin American Library Materials (Madison, WI: Secretariat, Seminar on the Acquisition of Latin American Library Materials, Memorial Library, University of Wisconsin, Madison, 1983).

[21]Rolando Lacayo and Martha L. Lacayo de Arauz, eds., Decretos-leyes para gobierno de un país a través de una Junta de Gobierno de Reconstrucción Nacional (Managua: Rolando D. Lacayo, 1979--).

[22]Index to Latin American Legislation (Boston, MA: G. K. Hall, 1950--). Latest cumulation covers up to 1975.

[23]Ellen G. Schaffer, "A Selective Guide to Law Related Publications of Latin America and the Caribbean," International Journal of Law Libraries, 6:1 (1978), 75-90.

[24]The Texas International Law Journal, Special Centennial Issue: "Law in Latin America," 1984.

[25]Charles Szladits, A Bibliography on Foreign and Compara-tive Law: Books and Articles in English (Dobbs Ferry, NY: Oceana, published for the Parker School of Foreign and Compara-tive Law, Columbia University, 1953--).

[26]The American Series of Foreign Penal Codes is published by Fred B. Rothman & Co., Littleton, CO.

[27]Kenneth R. Simmonds, ed., Commercial, Business and Trade Laws (Dobbs Ferry, NY: Oceana. Loose-leaf binders by country or region.

[28]International Labour Office, Legislative Series (Geneva: ILO, 1919--).

[29]Foreign Tax Law Association, Inc., P.O. Box 340, Alachua, FL 32615.

[30]M. A. García Caballero, "Guatemala: An Overview of the 1983 Tax Reform," Bulletin for International Fiscal Documentation, 38:3 (1984), 124.

[31]Bulletin of Legal Developments (London: The British Institute of International and Comparative Law, 1966--).

[32]Business Latin America (New York, NY: Business International Corporation, 1966--).

[33]Latin American Newsletters, Ltd., Boundary House, 91-93 Charterhouse Street, London EC1M 6LN, United Kingdom. Latin American Weekly Report and regional reports for Mexico and Central America, the Caribbean, Andean countries, Brazil, and the Southern Cone countries.

[34]Integración Latinoamericana (Buenos Aires: Instituto para la Integración de América Latina). Cerrito 264, 1010 Buenos Aires, Argentina.

[35]Grupo Andino: Carta Informativa de la Junta del Acuerdo de Cartagena. Junta del Acuerdo de Cartagena, Paseo de la República 3895, San Isidro, Lima, Peru.

[36]Organization of American States, General Secretariat, Mining and Petroleum Legislation of Latin America and the Caribbean (Dobbs Ferry, NY: Oceana, 1981--).

[37]International Bureau of Fiscal Documentation and Bomchil, Pinheiro, Goodrich, Claro and Lavalle. Corporate Taxation in Latin America (Amsterdam IBFD, 1975--).

[38]Salvador Miranda, "Dos and Don'ts When Acquiring Documents from Latin America and the Caribbean," Bulletin of the Florida Chapter of the Special Libraries Association, 15:2 (April, 1983), 82-86.

9. THE USE OF LATIN AMERICAN LEGAL MATERIALS IN THE UNITED STATES

Igor I. Kavass

The preceding papers discuss the many difficulties of identifying and acquiring South American legal materials. Of course, some of these difficulties may be directly related to the relatively low demand for such materials in the United States. In measuring the extent of the demand it is necessary to distinguish between the practice of law and academic legal research.

In legal practice the need for the texts of foreign laws is predicated upon the existence of a clientele with problems that are based on such laws. Only where the foreign laws are relevant to the solution of a problem will an attorney examine and analyze them, and even then it is likely that the problem may be referred by the United States attorney to a colleague in the particular foreign country whose greater familiarity with the law of that country may render more competent advice. It is not just a matter of language (though few attorneys in the United States can read or converse in languages other than English) or of knowledge of a foreign legal system. Professional responsibility dictates that an attorney should not attempt to interpret laws of a country where he does not practice. Although statistical data are not available, observations are sufficiently accurate to support the hypothesis that very few attorneys in the United States (and then only in the larger law firms with extensive international practices) require Latin American legal materials for their professional work.

Since academic research frequently results in publications, the data on the demand for Latin American legal materials in law schools and other centers of legal research are more easily accessible. To test the scope of this demand the following bibliographic sources were surveyed for the five-year period 1980–1984:

Szladits, Charles. A Bibliography on Foreign and Comparative Law: Books and Articles in English. Parker School Studies in Foreign and Comparative Law. Dobbs Ferry, NY: Oceana, 1955--.

Index to Legal Periodicals. New York, NY: H. W. Wilson.

Current Index to Legal Periodicals. Seattle, WA: University of Washington Law Library and Washington Law Review.

Index to Foreign Legal Periodicals. London: Institute of Advanced Studies, University of London.

The survey was limited to scholarly activities of substantial length. For the whole of this period, only twenty-seven articles were identified as dealing either with Latin American law in general or specifically with the laws of individual Latin American countries. The citations for these articles are given in the bibliography that follows, pages 68-70.

Upon examining the texts of these articles, the following general findings could be reported:

Subject Matter

More than 80 percent of the articles discuss commercial and investment law issues. The remainder are mostly political in nature; for example, human rights, the Falkland Islands controversy, Organization of American States policy.

Geographic Coverage

About one-third of the articles deal with Latin America in general. The rest are concerned with legal developments in specific countries. Surprisingly, there is relatively little current writing about Mexican law (there was greater scholarly interest in Mexican law in the two prior decades, when several treatises on the legal system of that country were published in English in the United States).

Character of Articles

They are mostly technical in nature and focus on a professional readership of attorneys and other law specialists.

Length of Articles

As might be expected, the length varies widely depending on the purpose of the article. C. Correa's "Transfer of Technology in Latin America," at 21 pages, is often cited and seems to be important. J. Rowle's massive two-part "Agrarian Reform in Costa Rica" is by far the longest at 231 pages.

Origin of Journals

Nearly all of the international and transnational law journals carry articles on Latin American topics, but Lawyer of the Americas is the most focused on the area. The Journal of World Trade Law and Law and Policy in International Business also consistently deal with the region, as does the Texas International Law Journal.

Identity of Researchers

Of the twenty-seven authors, thirteen are law professors or are associated with law schools either in the United States or in Latin America. Eleven others are currently in private practice, and two are law students. One, J. Jova, "Private Investment in Latin America," is a career diplomat (former ambassador to OAS and Honduras). Four writers either work in or have close ties to Latin America. For example, J. Ritch is an American-trained lawyer practicing in Mexico City; conversely, R. German is Peruvian-trained and working in New York.

Number of Sources Cited in the Footnotes

Of the ten articles selected for further analysis of sources, four average more than six footnotes per page. Such bare numbers have limited relevance, however, since a large number of citations per page indicates repeat citations of a small number of sources.

The number of actual sources cited varies according to the intent and format of the article. For example, in G. Cabanellas and W. Etzrodt, "The New Argentine Antitrust Law," 150 of 174 footnotes are to the Argentine Law itself. Conversely, R. Radway's "Next Decade in Latin America" includes a wide variety of primary and secondary sources.

Around one-third of the footnotes in any given article are explanatory or discursive. Since the articles deal with foreign topics, the authors frequently feel compelled to define terms, analyze foreign governmental and business practices, and spell out differences in relevant law and legal systems.

Nature of Sources Cited in the Footnotes

Very few of the articles are balanced between English and foreign language sources. D. Murray's "Drafts, Promissory Notes and Checks" (fourteen English, eleven Spanish), is the notable exception. Otherwise, the average article is about 90 percent either way, that is, dominated by English or Spanish sources.

Most U.S. researchers seem to depend on translations of Latin American laws; see, for example, G. Wilner, "The Transfer of Technology to Latin America."

The disciplinary perspective of an article also affects the nature of the sources used. For example, P. Schmidt's "Foreign Investment in Cuba" depends heavily on U.S. analyses of the Cuban economy, whereas W. D'Zurrilla's historical analysis, "Cuba's 1976 Socialist Constitution and the Fidelista Interpretation of Cuban Constitutional History," cites Cuban sources extensively, and especially the writings of Fidel Castro.

Writers with ties to Latin America cite predominantly Spanish or Portuguese secondary sources. Writers without such ties rely on secondary sources in the English language. Judging by the sources cited there are very few translations of Latin American legal publications; for example, laws or articles, from Spanish into English. Correa's article, originally published in Spanish, is a notable exception.

The survey leads to the conclusion that the demand for Latin American legal materials in the United States is relatively small and sporadic. When the demand occurs, it is usually directed toward materials dealing with topics that are concerned with the international affairs or economic situation at that particular time. There is nothing in the publishing pattern of the past five years to indicate a systematic approach to research. In these circumstances, the building of specialized Latin American law collections is very difficult. In order to have viable research resources it becomes necessary either to acquire every Latin American legal publication or to jump from subject to subject and country to country in the hope that some of the materials may turn out to be relevant for research. The analysis of the periodical literature on Latin American law also suggests that there is little communication between Latin American and United States legal scholars.

BIBLIOGRAPHY

Selected Articles on Latin American Law
in Periodicals in English since 1980

Cabanellas, Guillermo, and Wolf Etzrodt. "The New Argentine Antitrust Law: Competition as an Economic Policy Instrument." Journal of World Trade Law, 17 (1983), 34-53.

Caswell, Daniel P. "The Promised Land: Analysis of Environmental Factors of United States Investment in and Development of the Amazon Region in Brazil." Northwestern Journal of International Law and Business, 4 (1982), 517-550.

Correa, C. M. "Transfer of Technology in Latin America: A Decade of Control." Journal of World Trade Law, 15 (1981), 388-409.

Dahl, E., and Alejandro M. Garro. "Cuba's System of International Commercial Arbitration: A Convergence of Soviet and Latin American Trends." Lawyer of the Americas, 15 (1984), 441-466.

D'Zurilla, W. T. "Cuba's 1976 Socialist Constitution and the Fidelista Interpretation of Cuban Constitutional History." Tulane Law Review, 56 (1981), 1223-1288.

Fix Zamudio, Hector. "The Writ of Amparo in Latin America." Lawyer of the Americas, 13 (1981), 361-391.

French, Jan Hoffman. "Brazil's Profit Remittance Law: Reconciling Goals in Foreign Investments." Law and Policy in International Business, 14 (1982), 399-451.

German, Rafael. "Latin American Antitrust." Lawyer of the Americas, 14 (1982), 1-22.

Ietswaart, Heleen F. P. "Labor Relations Litigation: Chile, 1970-1972." Law and Society Review, 16 (1981-82), 625-668.

Jova, Joseph J., et al. "Private Investment in Latin America: Renegotiating the Bargain." Texas International Law Journal, 19 (1984), 3-32.

Leibman, Morris I., et al. "Latin American Law Symposium, December 11-12, 1981." California Western International Law Journal, 12 (1982), 397-510.

Leiseca, Sergio, and Thomas W. Studwell. "Latin American Accounts Receivable." Business Lawyer, 39 (1984), 495-519.

Long, C. T. "Caribbean Banking Subsidiaries and the International Banking Act of 1978." International Lawyer, 15 (1981), 687-707.

Marti, M. M. "Latin American Tax Law Update: 1980." Lawyer of the Americas, 13 (1981), 486-546.

Murray, Daniel E. "Drafts, Promissory Notes and Checks: A Comparison of Civilian, Quasi-Civilian and Non-Civilian Suggestions." Lawyer of the Americas, 15 (1983), 211-306.

Norberg, C. R. "Recent Developments in Inter-American Commercial Arbitration." Case Western Reserve Journal of International Law, 13 (1981), 107-117.

Pinheiro Neto, J. M., and Irene Dias da Silva. "Incentives for Investment in Brazil." Case Western Reserve Journal of International Law, 13 (1981), 123-139.

Radway, Robert J. "Antitrust, Technology Transfers and Joint Ventures in Latin American Development. Lawyer of the Americas, 15 (1983), 47-70.

_____. "The Next Decade in Latin America: Anticipating the Future from the Past." Case Western Reserve Journal of International Law, 13 (1981), 3-35.

Radway, Robert J., and Franklin T. Hoet-Linares. "Venezuela Revisited: Foreign Investment, Technology, and Related Issues." Vanderbilt Journal of Transnational Law, 15 (1982), 1-45.

Ritch, James E., Jr. "Legal Aspects of Lending to Mexican Borrowers." North Carolina Journal of International Law and Commercial Regulation, 7 (1982), 315-330.

Rosenn, Keith S. "Trends in Brazilian Regulation of Business." Lawyer of the Americas, 13 (1981), 169-209.

_____. "Regulation of Foreign Investment in Brazil: A Critical Analysis." Lawyer of the Americas, 15 (1983), 307-365.

Rowles, James P. "Law and Agrarian Reform in Costa Rica: The Legislative Phase." Lawyer of the Americas, 14 (1982): Part I, 149-257; Part II, 399-522.

Schmidt, Patrick L. "Foreign Investment in Cuba: A Preliminary Analysis of Cuba's New Joint Venture Law." Law and Policy in International Business, 15 (1983), 689-710.

Skola, T. J. "An Update on Brazilian Trading Companies and Export Credit." Lawyer of the Americas, 13 (1981), 421-426.

Wilner, G. M. "The Transfer of Technology to Latin America." Vanderbilt Journal of Transnational Law, 14 (1981), 269-279.

Collection and Organization of Primary Source Materials

‒

10. COLLECTION AND ORGANIZATION
OF PRIMARY RESOURCES

Marilyn P. Whitmore

Original/Primary Sources

Manuscript libraries collecting primary sources have been multiplying during the last four decades with extraordinary rapidity. This proliferation of manuscript libraries and archives has resulted in the preservation of more of this nation's written records than at any other time in our history, but growth has also created problems. A few decades ago the erection of a bell tower was the status symbol for the college or university. In the 1960s the status symbol became the possession of a manuscript library, or at least a college or university archive. Not only academic institutions but businesses, religious bodies, and government units are creating archives or expanding manuscript repositories in ever-increasing numbers. The new institutions are, however, very different from their illustrious forerunners, such as the Newberry and Bancroft libraries. Since most of the important documents and papers of the past centuries have already found their way into the hands of institutions, the attention of the newer institutions is focused either on more obscure materials or on the very recent past.

How does a manuscript library differ from an archive? Archives are the permanent records of a body of either a public or private character. An archival institution's first responsibility is to the agency which created the records and which may have further use for them for administrative or historical purposes. Preservation for researchers and scholars is only incidental. A manuscript library exists to serve the scholar, the researcher, and the student and collects papers and records of individuals and organizations that are not necessarily related to its institution. Its wide variety of materials, coming from a multiplicity of sources, makes its needs very different from those of an archival institution. There are, however, areas of commonality. Actually, "archives" has become a generic term that represents both archives and manuscripts because many of the manuscript library's materials are or resemble archival records. Thus, many of the archivists' techniques prove valuable to the manuscript librarian. The primary purpose of an archives or manuscript repository is to appraise, collect, preserve, arrange, describe, and make accessible those materials having permanent historical, legal, fiscal, administrative, or informational value. Archival or manuscript holdings may include textual, cartographic, audiovisual, and machine-readable records as well as prints, paintings, photographs, and artifacts.

Who Should Collect and What Should Be Collected

Well thought out, carefully drawn goals and objectives are fundamental to the successful development of any archive or manuscript collection, regardless of its size. There are, however, many manuscript libraries that collect materials regardless of whether they have any relationship to one another or even have any research value. Encouraged by professional historians seeking resources for their graduate students, academic institutions and even undergraduate colleges have made this mistake. Unplanned, indiscriminate collecting of manuscripts by any institution is not in the best interest of scholarship or even of the institution itself. The primary purpose of a manuscript collection should be to serve the world of scholarship, and this should determine its collecting policies.

Other factors to be considered seriously in establishing collection policy are the library's geographical location and its proximity to other manuscript collections, the parent institution supporting it, available financial resources, and the space and staff it has or can expect to have. The collection theme or subject may be limited to the parent institution's records, special subjects, geographic areas, time periods, or types of materials. The kinds of materials to be collected will determine the method of collecting. A written collection policy will prove helpful in turning down unwanted materials diplomatically and may be the first step in eliminating those items acquired indiscriminately in the past.

Conflict of interest can cause problems when a manuscript collection is part of a large library system. There is the danger that book-cataloging methods may be imposed on manuscripts or that book circulation policies may be applied to the use of manuscripts or in determining budget allocations. The specialists responsible for the management of manuscripts must clearly recognize the fundamental differences in treatment and use between published books and primary resources and must successfully interpret this difference to higher administrative levels.

The task of appraising materials is one of the most important responsibilities for the archivist/curator. The collection policy sets the general guidelines. The archivist/curator must then determine whether specific materials have sufficient value to warrant the time, space, and money necessary to preserve, arrange, and make them accessible. Only materials having permanent historical, legal, fiscal, administrative, or informational value should be considered archival. Experience, good judgment, and knowledge of the present holdings assist in appraising materials in light of the collection's purpose and goals.

Principles of Arrangement

Provenance and respect des fonds, or original order, have evolved as the major canons of archival theory from which archival procedures have derived. Until rather recently, archives and manuscripts were considered so dissimilar that applying the same principles to both was considered impractical. However, the increase in volume of nineteenth- and twentieth-century records and manuscripts has made these principles essentially mandatory.

In modern usage, the principle of provenance requires that records be maintained in the archives or manuscript repository according to the office or administrative entity that created and accumulated the records in the conduct of its business. The agency of creation has been extended to include the person, family, or other source of personal papers. In other words, there should be no intermingling of papers from different manuscript groups. It is unacceptable, for example, to pull letters from or to a particular individual which may exist in three or four different manuscript groups and bring them together either in one original or artificial group for whatever purpose.

The second principle, maintaining records in the original order used by the office or agency that created them, is less rigid in application. Concern for original order in an archival record group should be exercised, but with personal papers which may or may not systematically reflect the activity of their creator, the archivist/curator must impose on a disarrayed collection an order based on a combination of archival principles, manuscript techniques, and research needs. A custodian of an archival record group which was created for its documentation or use may lean toward the restoring of original order. On the other hand, an archivist/curator whose collections are primarily for research purposes might decide to impose a new order or arrangement upon that which reveals little of the creator's personality or is difficult for researchers to use. Whatever the circumstances, archivists and curators must examine and analyze the records carefully before either disrupting the original order in cases where such order exists, restoring original order where no apparent order is perceived, or modifying the order where there is a viable accessible order.

Organization

The organization of an archival collection is based on arrangement and description, which are closely related. Arrangement is personal to each collection, reflecting the activity, and occasionally even the personality, of the curator. The essence of arrangement is that each document has a proper, specific place. Description systematizes information about the holdings and provides the researcher with the means of access to germane materials.

Arrangement

The arrangement of primary resources varies in degree on different levels: repository, record group/collection and subgroup, series, file unit, and document. This process is described in an article, "Archival Arrangement: Five Different Operations at Five Different Levels," which appeared in the American Archivist in 1964.

When collections arrive in a state of chaos the archivist/ curator must be prepared to formulate an order that is both logical and comparable to the arrangement of collections maintained in their original order. Some logical order may be developed from chronology, topic, function of the creator, or type of material. Series based on *chronology* establish periods such as years or decades into which documents can be placed solely on the basis of their date of publication. For example:

> Correspondence, 1900-1909
> > Letters received, 1900-1908
> > Letters sent, 1901-1909

This is especially applicable for a few hundred items or less. Forming series around *topic* is the least advisable approach since many documents discuss more than one topic. It should be used only when the topics are indisputable. Arrangement by *function or activity of the creator* is preferred because it best illuminates the evidential values in the records and is probably close to original order. In this arrangement, documents that clearly relate to distinct activities of the creator, such as correspondence or legal documents concerning the construction of a building, or the minutes and financial records reflecting a person's service as treasurer of an organization, are grouped together. Arrangement by *type of material* segregates the documents by their physical characteristics. The basic types are:

correspondence	minutes and diaries
financial documents	photographic material
legal documents	printed material
literary productions and reports	scrapbooks
maps, charts, etc.	sound recordings

Description

The other component of organization is description. That implies *finding aids* that establish physical and intellectual control over archives and manuscripts. The control provides (1) essential information about the records, (2) knowledge of the information in the records, and (3) the holdings themselves. The more

---

*Oliver W. Holmes, "Archival Arrangement: Five Different Operations at Five Different Levels," American Archivist, 27:1 (Jan., 1964), 21-42.

detailed this control information, the more exact a researcher can be in a request for material and the less staff time need be diverted to reference and retrieval.

The basic finding aid is an *inventory* which includes (1) an overview, (2) a biographical sketch or agency history, (3) a scope and content note, and (4) a series description which reveals the actual arrangement of the collection.

An *in-house reference aid* is essential to access the collections and their inventories because searching numerous inventories is slow and tedious work. An in-house aid is analogous to a computer data bank. It focuses on the subject content of all the collections in a given repository, enabling staff and researchers to survey these extensive holdings for material relevant to their specific needs. Most repositories have been using a card catalog; the form for recording arrangement and content data was patterned closely on book catalog cards. With the basic information in card format, a list of subject headings can be created. Repositories often find that standard subject headings are too general. The archivist/curator not only needs the standard subject headings, which offer broad directions to a search, but also should supply the specific names, places, and events that the user more often seeks.

For integrating and centralizing in-house reference service, no finding aid has improved as yet on the card system. This system was developed in the 1950s for uniform recording of the National Union Catalog of Manuscript Collections and provided for the following data elements: name of the collection or main entry; nature of the collection or title showing whether papers, records, or collection and with inclusive dates; statement of the occupation or type of activity of the creator; physical description; scope and content note.

Because the collection so laboriously processed will be used only if pains are taken to inform potential users of its existence, *external reference aids* are also important. For seeking material by subject, especially if the researcher is unsure which repositories might hold certain material or data on a given topic, the best source is the National Union Catalog of Manuscript Collections (NUCMC) which describes significant individual collections.

With the publication of NUCMC, one may ask why a repository should publish a guide to its own holdings. First, NUCMC does not include all collections. The requirements are too rigid and its space is too limited to permit full coverage of any sizable repository's holdings. Second, NUCMC can be used only through its index while a repository guide can be organized topically, chronologically, or alphabetically. Third, a comprehensive in-house guide is extremely useful for serving researchers both in person and by mail; it can save a great deal of needle-in-haystack hunting.

A manuscript library or repository has an obligation to pub-
licize its holdings in an many ways as possible. No manuscript
library deserves to exist if it is unable to inform scholars of its
resources.

BIBLIOGRAPHY

Bordin, Ruth B., and Robert M. Warner. The Modern Manuscript
    Library. New York, NY: Scarecrow Press, 1966.

Gracy, David B. Archives and Manuscripts: Arrangement and
    Description. Chicago, IL: Society of American Archivists,
    1977.

Holmes, Oliver W. "Archival Arrangement: Five Different
    Operations at Five Different Levels." American Archivist, 27:1
    (Jan., 1964), 21–42.

Zabrosky, Frank A. "Appraisal and Arrangement of Textual
    Records." In A Manual of Archival Techniques, Roland M.
    Baumann, ed. Harrisburg, PA: Pennsylvania Historical and
    Museum Commission, 1979.

11. LATIN AMERICAN HISTORICAL PHOTOGRAPHS IN THE LIBRARIES OF THE UNIVERSITY OF TEXAS AT AUSTIN AND TULANE UNIVERSITY

Thomas Niehaus

Introduction

Collecting Latin American historical and documentary photographs is a relatively new and limited activity in U.S. research libraries. Only a few institutions are actively collecting such material. I am aware of five libraries that do so: They are the Library of Congress, the University of Arizona, the University of Texas Library, the Peabody Museum of Harvard University, and the Tulane University Library.

The Library of Congress has about 15,000 photographs of Latin American art and architecture. They are mounted on boards and housed in file cabinets in the basement of the library. It is set up as a working collection for scholars in art and architecture.

The Center for Creative Photography at the University of Arizona in Tucson has approximately 20,000 photographs in the Pal Keleman Collection on art and architecture of South America. This collection was acquired in the late 1970s. In addition, there are several other collections of Latin American photographs at Arizona. The emphasis in this collection is on artistic photographs. In the other repositories mentioned here the emphasis is on documentary photos.

The Benson Latin American Collection at the University of Texas has approximately 18,000 historical photographs. They cover all areas of Latin America, but concentrate on Mexico and Brazil. The strongest subject area is art and architecture.

The Peabody Museum of Harvard University has about 50,000 Latin American historical photographs. Most of the collection consists of 42,000 images (negatives and their prints) relating to archaeology in southern Mexico and northern Central America. These were given to the Museum in 1957 by the Carnegie Institution of Washington. The Museum also has 4,000 nineteenth-century contact prints, 2,000 slides, and about 2,000 negatives of artifacts in the Museum, all of which relate to Latin America.

Tulane University has about 22,000 Latin American historical photographs. Half of them are housed in the Latin American

Author's Note. An earlier draft of this paper was read at the meeting of the Southern Council on Latin American Studies (SCOLAS) in Austin, Texas, on March 22, 1980.

Library, and the other half are in the Middle American Research
Institute. The majority of the photos are on Indian life in Mexico
and Central America, but there are also significant collections on
Peruvian art and architecture.

It is because Latin American historial photographs have been
recognized as an important source for historical evidence only in
recent years that there are so few repositories that are making a
serious attempt to collect these photos. But the importance of
this work cannot be underestimated, because in some Latin
American countries the cultural agencies are not making a strong
effort to preserve historial photographs. Examples of countries
that do have extensive, well-preserved photographic archives are
Mexico, Brazil, and Argentina.

The purpose of this paper is to describe in some detail
the Latin American photographic archives in the Benson Latin
American Collection at the University of Texas at Austin and at
Tulane University.

The University of Texas Collection

Many scholars are aware of the importance of the García
Collection which formed the nucleus of the Texas holdings in
Latin American books and manuscripts. But the García Collection
also contains 3,169 photographs. Most of these were taken in
1910 during the centenario of Mexican independence. They are
photos of civilian, military, and church personalities who were
involved in various ceremonies during the celebration of the
centenary. It includes photos of expositions at such places as
the Museo Nacional and fiestas held during the centenary. For
example, there are 96 photos of the Indian women of Tehuantepec
in their native costume. There are 24 photos of General Felix
Díaz in Veracruz in 1912, and 37 photos of European historical
figures of the early twentieth century.

The Benson Collection also has the John McAndrew Photographic Archive, containing about 6,000 photographs of Mexican
art and architecture, and consisting of mostly sixteenth-century
religious architecture. Many of the photographs have been published in John McAndrew's book, The Open Air Churches of
Sixteenth-Century Mexico, 1965.

The Brazilian Photographic Archive contains 3,500 photographs. Of these, 2,300 are of Brazilian civil and religious
architecture, mostly baroque and rococo, photographed by Hans
Mann. Texas also has 582 photographs of Bolivian baroque architecture, mostly in La Paz and Copacabana, also photographed by
Hans Mann. There are some 386 photographs of Peruvian colonial
art and architecture, comprised mainly of churches and some
popular art. These, too, were taken by Hans Mann.

The St. John del Rey Mining Company Archive photographs
contain 1,900 photos of a mine in Minas Gerais, Brazil. Most
were taken in the period 1890-1904. There are twelve albums of

photographs on the Morro Velho gold mine, and the nearby city of Novo Lima. The photos illustrate mining operations, equipment, transportation, black miners, workshops, offices, and so on. They are included with the mining company's archive of annual reports and account books.

The Bartlett Collection of Mexican hacienda photos contains 890 items, including some slides, drawings, and sketches. Taken in the period 1952-1972, these photos document various Mexican haciendas and the working and living conditions on them.

The Chase Littlejohn Photographic Collection contains 295 photos, many taken during the Mexican Revolution (1910-1920). Littlejohn was a mining engineer in Mexico.

The George I. Sánchez collection of photographs totals 277 items. Almost all are of rural schools in New Mexico in 1934 and 1935. These photos document the poor conditions in schools and housing for Mexican-Americans in that area. There are also 30 photos of Mexican-American migrant workers' camps that document poor housing conditions.

The Tabasco Rubber Plantation photo collection has 137 images. They are views of three rubber plantations in the state of Tabasco, Mexico. There are photos of owners, administrators, and laborers. Most were taken in the early twentieth century.

Some of the most important photographs in the entire Texas collection are in the Taracena Flores Collection. This collection of Central American materials contains about 400 photographs, most of them taken in the late nineteenth or early twentieth century in Guatemala City. They show church officials, politicians, and other important personages. The photographers were not Guatemalans but rather traveling photographers from other countries, including G. A. Howley and E. Herbruger. Many of the pictures in the collection are so-called cartes-de-visite, a European tradition that was carried to Latin America in the nineteenth century. Collected in great numbers by people in Guatemala, Mexico, and other Latin American countries, these small, pocket-sized photos of politicians and ecclesiastical personages contain biographies on the reverse side and served as a form of self-promotion. The phenomenon of the cartes-de-visite in Latin America has been studied by Keith McElroy in his 1977 dissertation on the history of photography in nineteenth-century Peru. McElroy found that Peruvians spent a very high percentage of their income purchasing large numbers of cartes-de-visite. It seems to be a phenomenon closely allied to the issue of personalismo in Latin America. The Taracena Flores Collection contains 20 cartes-de-visite from Guatemala, 70 from Mexico, 35 from Europe, and 30 from the United States.

The Tulane University Collection

Tulane University has 40 collections of Latin American historical and documentary photographs with a total of about

22,000 images. About half of these are contained in the Latin American Library; the other half are in the Middle American Research Institute.

The following is a list of the collections in the Middle American Research Institute (MARI).

	Number of photographs
Photographs of archaeological sites and artifacts, Indian daily life, pottery making, Indian dances, folkloric activities. Arranged by country and then by Indian village. Photos taken between 1920 and 1950.	
1. Mexico	2,350
2. Guatemala	950
3. Honduras	375
4. Peru	75
5. Belize	50
6. Venezuela	35
7. Ecuador	40
8. Panama (includes Panama Canal)	55

MARI archaeological and anthropological expedition photographs:

9. John Geddings Grey Expedition (1928) to Chiapas, Mexico.	30
Photos of Indian daily life.	
10. Matilda Geddings Gray Expedition (1933) to Guatemala.	150
Photos on Indian daily life, especially textiles and costumes.	
11. Dimick Expedition (1940) to Mexico.	45
Archaeology.	

Other MARI collections:

12. United States Indian Photograph Collection	400
Mostly Indians from the Southwest and California; some from Pennsylvania, Ohio, etc. Photos on daily life of Indians, native dress, food, textiles, pottery, dances, and musical instruments. Taken in 1920-1950.	
13. Julia K. Lowe Photograph Collection	85
Mexican cities, colonial buildings, and railroads; 1930s.	

		Number of photographs

14. Kaehler Photograph Collection — 20
    Portraits of Guatemalan Indians; 1930s.

15. E. Wyllys Andrews IV Photograph Collection — 500
    Archaeological sites in Mexico, especially the Yucatan; 1930-1950.

16. Loring M. Hewen Photograph Collection — 500
    Archaeological sites in the Yucatan; also some sites in Central America. Portraits of Indians; 1940-1960.

17. Hans Namuth Photograph Collection — 75
    Mexican Indian daily life and folklore; 1940s.

18. Gordon Abbott Photograph Collection — 100
    Mexican colonial architecture and Indian daily life; 1940-1960.

19. Central American Aerial Survey Photograph Collection — 75
    A complete set of photos from the 1930 Aerial Expedition to Central America, produced by Fairchild Aerial Surveys, Inc., New York.

20. MARI Museum Artifacts Photograph Collection — 155
    Middle American artifacts.

21. Mexican and Central American Manuscripts Photograph Collection — 60
    Photos of various important manuscripts offered for sale to MARI from 1924 to 1960. Mostly on Mexico and Central America. The location of the manuscripts not purchased by MARI is no longer known. The manuscripts purchased are now in the Tulane Latin American Library.

22. Collection of glass plate negatives on Indian daily life in Mexico and the U.S. Southwest; 1880-1915. — 850

23. Collection of film negatives for which there are no prints in any of the above collections — 3,250
    Subject matter: Archaeology and ethnography of Mexico and Central America.

	Subtotal of items in MARI	10,225

The following is a list of photographic collections in the Latin American Library at Tulane University.

Number of
photographs

24. Emilio Harth-Terre Photograph Collection   4,332

Peruvian colonial architecture; buildings dated 1537-1800. This is one of the most complete collections of its kind: documents doorways, grills, columns, churches, etc. Its detail is very useful for the architectural historian, as many of the buildings were torn down in the renovation of Lima in the 1950s. Most photos taken from 1940 to 1960. This is the Latin American Library's largest documentary photo collection. Harth-Terre is a Peruvian architect and architectural historian who was in charge of the preservation of colonial buildings after the 1940 earthquake. He is not a photographer, but was given these photographs for his own use during the restoration.

25. Abraham Guillén Photograph Collection   863

Peruvian archaeology, ethnography, and colonial architecture. Includes pre-Hispanic art objects, folk dances, regional costumes, and scenes from the Vicos Project (1955-1965). Guillén's archive of 14,000 negatives is housed in the Instituto Nacional de Cultura in Lima. From 1932 to 1975 Guillén was head of the Department of Photography in the National Archaeological Museum, now known as the Museum of Peruvian Culture. His photos have been used in books, encyclopedias, and other general publications on Peru. His are perhaps the most well-known of all Peruvian photographs, although often he was not given credit for his work. The standard photos on Peru that appeared in national and international magazines from 1950 to 1970 are often Guillén's work, even though his name does not appear on them.

26. Martín Chambi Photograph Collection   70

This is Tulane's finest exhibit-quality collection. Chambi was one of Latin America's most famous artistic photographers. He worked in his studio in Cuzco, Peru, from 1925 to 1965, producing an archive of 16,000 negatives,

many of them on glass plates. The archive is
still in Cuzco, and is well cared for by his
sister Julia. Chambi often ventured into the
Peruvian countryside to photograph the high-
land Indians. The Tulane exhibit collection is
on Peruvian Indians, high society in Cuzco,
and portraits of famous Peruvians.

27. Eadweard Muybridge Photograph Collection   142

Central American scenes taken in the 1870s
when Muybridge was employed by a shipping
company. He is a famous pioneer photographer known especially for his motion
studies. This collection documents ports,
cities, and plantations in Central America.
The collection was a gift from Sidney D.
Markman.

28. Sidney D. Markman Photograph Collection   2,497

Eighteenth-century colonial architecture of
Antigua, Guatemala, and of Mexico City.
Photos used as the basis for Markman's book
on Antigua architecture. Some photos of
twentieth-century Ecuadorian architecture.
All taken in the 1960s.

29. Ephraim George Squier Photograph Collection   300

Scenes of Indian life taken in Honduras in the
1850s and in Peru in the 1860s. There are
very few original Squier photos in existence,
which has made this collection of great
interest for scholars. These photos were
used as the basis for the engravings that
illustrate Squier's travel books on Central
America and Peru.

30. Mitchell Denburg Photograph Collection   600

Photos of Guatemala documenting nineteenth-
century farming equipment, twentieth-century
city and rural life, and the government and
church leaders of Guatemala. Taken from
1979 to 1983. Denburg's work is sponsored
by the Centro de Investigaciones Regionales de
Mesoamérica (CIRMA), Antigua, Guatemala.
CIRMA and Tulane have commissioned
Mr. Denburg to document Guatemalan daily
life, and especially aspects of Indian life and
customs.

Number of
photographs

31. Juan Yas and Juan D. Noriega Photograph
Collection   70

Yas was the first Guatemalan photographer,
and Noriega was his assistant. Almost all
photos are from the period 1880-1940. Most
are portraits of Guatemalans. This collection
was discovered by Mitchell Denburg in
Antigua, Guatemala. The collection was given
to Tulane by CIRMA (see preceding entry),
and is a traveling exhibit in the United
States, sponsored by CIRMA. CIRMA also
exhibits this collection in Antigua, Guatemala,
where it has its offices.

32. Judith Sandoval Photograph Collection   720

Nicaraguan colonial churches, archaeological
sites, contemporary rural buildings and work
places. Includes details of farm machinery
and rural machinery used in sugar cane
production. Sandoval is an American photographer who took these photos in 1974.

33. Abbye Gorin Photograph Collection   242

Archaeological sites in the Yucatan and Central America; pre-Columbian stone sculpture;
also some photos of Machu Picchu and of
architecture in Spain. Taken in the 1970s.

34. Ernest L. Crandall Photograph Collection   197

Archaeological and anthropological photos of
Mexico and Central America; taken on the
Carnegie Institution expeditions to Middle
America in 1924-1927.

35. Mexican Hacienda Photograph Collection   200

Hacienda buildings and lands; taken between
1960 and 1970.

36. Ronald Hilton Photograph Collection   100

General Latin American photos taken in the
1950s: city street scenes, modern buildings,
etc. Includes Cuba and the Spanish-American
War of 1898. In addition, there are 4,000
Latin American postcards from the 1950s.

		Number of photographs
37.	Rudolph Schuller Photograph Collection	1,000

Mexican photos taken during the Revolution, 1910–1920. Mexico City, archaeological sites, revolutionary armies, and Huastecan Indians.

38.	George Pepper Photograph Collection	620

Ethnographic photos of Indians in the U.S. Southwest, 1880–1910.

39.	Pan American Union Photograph Collection	99

Group portraits of Latin American intellectuals and government leaders who visited the Pan American Union in Washington, DC, in the period 1941–1946.

40.	Horst Janson Photograph Collection	300

Peruvian pre-Columbian stone figures and architecture; photos taken in the 1960s.

Subtotal of Latin American Library photos	12,352
Total Tulane University photographs	22,577

The Latin American Library at Tulane has prepared traveling exhibits of selected Peruvian photos from both the Harth-Terre and Guillén collections. In cooperation with CIRMA (Centro de Investigaciones Regionales de Mesoamérica), it has established a traveling exhibit of the Yas and Noriega photos on nineteenth-century Guatemala. The library has also exhibited the Chambi photographs at the New Orleans Museum of Art.

Scholarly Uses of Latin American Historical Photographs

Many Latin Americanists are just beginning to use photos in their research. I believe that not enough of this type of research is being done. The most obvious use of historical photos is by historians who want illustrations for their books. I would hope that the use of Latin American historical photographs would soon go beyond this level.

In the last ten years historians specializing in Latin America have done some very creative work in the use of notarial archives to study social history in the colonial period. This imaginative use of sources can also be done with historical photographs. For instance, a photo of a street in a small city in Latin America in the late nineteenth century can show forms of transportation, names of companies on buildings, styles of clothing, and many other types of information.

Photographs can also be used for propaganda purposes. Keith McElroy found that in nineteenth-century Peru some photos were altered to give false evidence of particular historical incidents. This use of photography as propaganda is a very important subject to be studied by historians and other interested scholars.

Anthropologists and art historians are two groups that can greatly benefit by the use of photographs. The art historian has a wealth of information at both Texas and Tulane. Their largest collections document thousands of colonial buildings in Latin America. Many of these buildings have been destroyed by earthquakes or modernization, and so the photographs are the only source of visual information about them. Anthropologists can use photographs to document folk dances, regional costumes, and life-styles of Latin American Indians. Archaeologists can use historical photographs to document archaeological sites at earlier periods, before restoration or vandalism.

Conclusion

The collection of Latin American historical photographs is a very significant development in the field of Latin American Studies today. It is an attempt to preserve some of the most important historical evidence available. There are photographic collections in Latin America that will be destroyed if someone does not find a way to preserve them, due to the fact that in some Latin American countries the cultural agencies do not have a strong orientation for preserving photographs. Usually, the best way to learn about a photographic collection from Latin America is from researchers in the field. They hear about the availability of a collection and, if we are lucky, do something about getting a library or archive to preserve it.

Just as the invention of printing in the fifteenth century opened up a whole new world of information for scholars and students, the invention of the camera in the nineteenth century has resulted in a tremendous amount of new visual information on Latin America. Those resources are just now beginning to be tapped.

BIBLIOGRAPHY

Camp, Roderic Ai. "Martín Chambi." Américas, 30 (March, 1978).

Horne, Jed. "A Culture Caught in Time: Photographs by Martín Chambi." Quest/79 (New York), 3:4 (June, 1979), 54-59.

McElroy, Douglas Keith. "The History of Photography in Peru in the Nineteenth Century." Ph.D. diss., University of New Mexico, 1977.

Collection Techniques:
Foreign Acquisition Field Trips

12. BOOK-BUYING TRIPS TO LATIN AMERICA: IDEAS AND SUGGESTIONS

Thomas Niehaus

Introduction

The purpose of this paper is to cover some of the practical aspects of book-buying trips to Latin America. The ideas and suggestions given here are based on personal experience on such trips. The advantages of these trips are not limited to the benefits of increased acquisitions for the library; the experience also gives the bibliographer a good feel for Latin American countries and much information is acquired about how to answer a variety of reference questions at one's home institution. For example, knowing that, in a given country, the Central Bank publishes better statistics than the Census Bureau is an important bit of information in answering reference questions related to statistics.

Preparing for the Trip

Reports of Previous Trips from Colleagues

Many librarians are required by their institutions to write reports on their buying trips to Latin America. These are in-house reports that are seldom published. At best, a summary may appear in the library's newsletter. Most people who have written such reports are very willing to share them with colleagues, but one must ask for them and know whom to ask. Contacts among the bibliographers in SALALM should be helpful in determining who has been on a recent trip to a particular country of interest.

Often these reports give names and addresses of specific persons contacted and whether or not the contact was fruitful. These lists can obviously save much time and avoid a lot of wasted effort in the field. Even one good report from the country of interest can make a big difference in one's effectiveness.

List of Exchange Partners

One's own library exchange program is a natural source of contacts. If the library does not have such a program, it is possible to obtain a list for a specific country by asking colleagues to photocopy and send their exchange addresses.

Some bibliographers confine the purpose of a trip to strengthening ties with exchange partners and trying to find new partners. This is a very good way to make the trip manageable. To attempt to buy books and to contact all one's exchange partners can be a huge job, especially if the trip includes visits to several countries. A common mistake made by people on their first trip is trying to do too much in a short time.

If the time is available, it is wise to write ahead to some exchange partners telling them of your proposed trip and the approximate day of arrival. This will help insure a good welcome, and it will give the contacts time to prepare for your visit.

Dealers' Lists as Sources of Contacts

An obvious way of obtaining the names of contacts is to review a dealer's list of recent titles for sale. This will provide a list of publishers. You may want to continue to buy through a dealer to insure a regular flow of new items from the country, but it is very useful to visit the publishers themselves and get an idea of the types of titles they plan to bring out in the future. Dealers' lists can also offer ideas for potential exchange partners, especially among the government agencies and university publishers.

Buddy System for the First Trip

I went on my first buying trip with a faculty member who had been going to the same Latin American countries every summer for many years. He had numerous contacts and gave me all sorts of detailed information on how to get around in the country. In each country we visited we would spend the first day together. He introduced me to his key contacts, and then on the second and third days of the visit we would each do our own tasks: he in the historical archives and I in the government agencies, bookstores, and the like.

During a recent book-buying trip I served as an experienced colleague for a fellow bibliographer who was on her first buying trip. Learning the ropes on the spot is a very efficient way of becoming an experienced book buyer in Latin America. I think that a buddy system of this kind can save the first-time traveler many headaches, and can make fellow bibliographers true colleagues.

Planning the Length of the Trip

The limits of one's endurance are learned only through experience. I have found that my limit is two weeks on a buying trip. The third week becomes wearing. If distance and expense dictate a longer trip, some rest periods, perhaps long weekends in a place of tourist interest, should be included.

Packing Materials for Shipping Books

On a typical trip I pack one suitcase with clothes and fill another with wrapping paper, twine, scissors, and pre-addressed shipping labels. These items are often difficult to obtain in an unfamiliar Latin American city, and valuable time can be wasted on a trip searching for them.

Incidentally, the best place to buy thick twine (or thin rope) in San José, Costa Rica, is in a leather store that sells saddles and lassos. Thin lassos make wonderful package rope. But it took me a lot of time and effort to discover that hardware stores in San José do not sell rope. Save time by bringing it along.

Finding Out about Customs Ahead of Time

One of the major problems on a buying trip can be getting shipments through customs. Each country has a different bureaucratic structure, and prior information about it will be very useful. Sometimes a bibliographer's in-house report of a trip will contain such information. Most often, however, it is obtained by word of mouth at SALALM meetings or in phone calls to someone who has made the trip before.

A typical pattern of customs requirements for shipping books out of a Latin American country is as follows: An export license must be obtained, often by having to take copies of the invoices to the Central Bank where the export license is issued. This means the usual waiting in long lines at the bank, and it can throw a trip off schedule very easily.

A typical difficulty in the process: One brings only the original invoices to the bank and does not want to leave them with the export license application. The bank does not have a photocopying service. One must find a copying machine, no mean feat in an unfamiliar Latin American city. Then back to the bank to wait in the long line again. It is very easy to lose a full day over such problems. The solution: Take multiple copies of invoices to the bank on the first trip.

An example of an air freight shipment by a group of bibliographers in June, 1983, in Managua: The customs officials at the airport required a letter signed by the government cabinet minister under whose jurisdiction customs fell, not easy to do since the minister was out of town. It took two full days of work to clear the shipment through customs, including many trips back and forth from the airport to the various ministries. But the bibliographers were experienced, had anticipated this problem, and had allowed time for it in their schedule. Nevertheless, the frustrations of these experiences cannot be eliminated despite advance planning.

Attempting to Buy for More than One Library

Several years ago it occurred to me that it is very inefficient to go to the trouble of ferreting out hard-to-find books in Latin America and then buy just one copy. It seemed to me that I should get three or four copies and provide them to other research libraries in the United States. I tried to organize a co-operative buying arrangement with four other libraries for obtaining Central American books. This occurred in the late 1970s when there were few reliable dealers in Central America, and librarians had to invent their own acquisitions methods. The theory was that each year or so one member of the group would go on a buying trip to Central America and buy for all.

This was all very well in theory, but there were fatal flaws in the system. First, it is very difficult for one person to arrange for the shipping of four times the books he would normally buy. The logistics are just too difficult. Also, the members could not share the task equitably because they did not go to Central America on a regular round-robin schedule. Luckily a system of good dealers evolved in Central America, so the acquisition problem was largely solved.

There are some solutions to the problem of buying for more than one library. On a 1983 trip to Managua I bought extra copies of books for the Library of Congress and solved the shipping problem by dropping them off at the U.S. Embassy in Managua for shipment to L.C. via the diplomatic pouch. I also bought third copies of some titles which seemed to be particularly hard to obtain, made of list of them when I returned to Tulane, and offered them to other U.S. libraries having an interest in that country's publications. Given the difficulties of multiple buying, perhaps this is the best compromise.

Bring Calling Cards

It is all-important to have a supply of calling cards along on the trip. Use them as an introduction upon arrival in an office reception area, for getting on mailing lists for exchange publications, and so forth. Everyone will ask for a card, and you will have a good collection of their cards on your return.

Take Along Lists of Titles

Lists of specific titles are especially useful on the trip. These lists might include out-of-print desiderata, serials whose subscriptions have lapsed, or needed back issues of serials.

Things to Do During the Trip
Planning Daily Contacts, Maps, Taxis

On arrival, get a good map of the city from a newsstand, bookstore, or the hotel lobby. Plot out the locations of contacts and exchange partners on the map. This will probably require the help of a taxi driver or a hotel employee. Having become familiar with the general sections of the city and the grouping of contacts in certain areas, hire a taxi driver. Consider hiring someone for the whole day, but perhaps try the first or second contact with individual taxis to see how it works. It is easy to get tied up at one spot for a long time.

On only one trip, in San Salvador, did I use public buses extensively. It was fun to learn the bus routes, but doing so used up a lot of valuable time. Taxis are by far the most efficient means of transportation.

The Usual Contacts: Government Agencies, Banks, Universities

Most contacts will be government agencies and universities: the Dirección General de Estadística y Censos, the Banco Central, the university presses, the university bookstores. In many Latin American countries the largest publisher is the cultural division of a major bank as, for example, in Quito, Ecuador.

Some Less-than-Usual Contacts: Newsstands, Airports

Let your imagination go while exploring the city for books, and do not overlook newsstands. Get samples of magazines and journals there as well as political ephemera, such as pamphlets on current issues, as these are very valuable for researchers. Airport bookstores may not look very impressive, but they often have valuable material. In Managua the two bookstalls at the airport handle a good variety of current publications.

Faculty Contacts at Universities

A few faculty members at your home institution may have some special contacts in a given country who can be useful for getting into the grapevine of the publications world. These faculty members may know of an institute in the university that is publishing just the kinds of things you want. They may also know a colleague whose library is for sale.

Shipping Methods: Post Office, Air Freight

In some countries the post office is reliable for shipping books. If so, it is obviously cheaper to use the mails than air freight. But in many Latin American countries, the postal service leaves much to be desired. If that is the case, air freight is definitely worth the extra expense. Too much time and money is spent on a trip to have the books lost in shipment. Take the safer way.

If air freight customs are difficult in a country, and only two or three boxes of books must be sent, consider taking them along as excess baggage to the next country if customs are easier there. I avoided the difficult chore of Nicaraguan air freight customs by taking my books with me to Costa Rica where the air freight customs were very simple.

Packaging Methods

If the regular mails are used, take the books to your hotel room and proceed to use the wrapping supplies you brought with you to make up the packages for shipment. It is best to do this at night when you cannot be out making contacts. If you decide to use air freight, it is best to find some boxes for the books since they will accept larger packages than will the post office. If you have a large quantity to send by air freight, ask someone at the hotel or at a publisher's office to recommend a company that will package the books and take them through air freight customs for you, but try to accompany the shipment personally to the air terminal.

The U.S. Embassy as a Source of Publishing Contacts

Some cultural affairs officers in U.S. embassies know the book trade in their countries and may be of help. If extra time is available in a country, try the U.S. embassy, but in general it is preferable to come prepared with all your own contacts.

Things to Do after the Trip

Tie Up All the Loose Ends and Correspondence

One returns from a trip with a list of things to do, for example, "Tell serials that such and such a journal has ceased," "Tell Prof. Jones that the university press in Costa Rica wants to do a translation of his book," "Send a sample of our Latin American Center's publications to Jaime in San Salvador." The list will go on and on. It is very easy to let these things slide. One approach to avoid this is to reserve the first two days after returning from a trip for tying up all these loose ends. Resist the temptation to open the stacks of mail that await you. Consider that the first two days back are still a part of the trip. Following through on the promises made to your contacts in Latin America will stand you in good stead when you write to them in the future asking for a favor.

Update Exchange Lists

Pull out all the new addresses and calling cards obtained on the trip and have a staff member send exchange questionnaires to the new exchange partners.

Book Buying Trips as "Learning Experiences"

Sometimes it is difficult for a bibliographer to justify the expense of a book-buying trip to a foreign country when proposing it to the library administration. One important thing to remember is that these are more than buying trips. They are learning trips in which one finds out how the country is organized, how the university is structured, how the government ministries work, and many other bits of information that are very useful in answering reference questions.

In one sense a major goal of a book-buying trip is to learn how to buy books intelligently after returning home. Learning firsthand the structure of book trade in a given country enables you to know where to look in the future for publications. If on your trip you learn that the Central Bank of a given country publishes more books on history and literature than the major universities, you will be better prepared to collect the items your library needs from that country.

The Importance of Bookdealers

Buying trips will never take the place of good bookdealers. In fact, if there is one thing to be learned on a buying trip it is that a good bookdealer in a foreign country is worth his weight in gold. One learns how difficult it is to ferret out books in Latin America, and how time-consuming and expensive it is. Occasional buying trips result in many extra books and keep one up to date on publishing trends, but it is the bookdealer who provides a regular series of lists or blanket order shipments that are the mainstay of a library's acquisitions program.

Conclusion

These ideas and suggestions should be useful for librarians who are going on their first acquisition trip to Latin America. It is a complicated business, but the first trip is also an adventure. Bibliographers should keep a list of their own ideas learned from experiences and pass them on to colleagues who will follow.

13. BOOK-COLLECTING TRIPS: A BRITISH VIEW

Patricia E. Noble

Although some British librarians had already visited various parts of Latin America before 1970 in order to establish or re-affirm contacts with postal suppliers and government departments and to set up or revive exchange agreements, I think I was probably the first to undertake a major collecting trip of the kind which had already been carried out by a number of North American bibliographers, that is, with the intention from the start of buying material for cash from whatever sources offered them. I suspect, however, that for several reasons there may be some significant differences between my book-collecting trips and those undertaken, as it seems to me, far more regularly and with much more clearly defined parameters, by U.S. librarians. I therefore propose to describe my own objectives, methods and experiences, in the hope that useful points of similarity or difference may emerge.

Most British Latin Americanists cannot hope to have collecting trips authorized at shorter intervals than about every two years, and funds do not normally stretch to visiting more than two or three countries at most on each occasion. The higher cost of travel, the lesser importance apparently attached to Latin American studies in the United Kingdom generally, and the fact that subject specialization amongst librarians is in itself a relatively recent development, are all factors which militate against the acceptance in British academic libraries of the importance of the collecting trip as a normal and regular part of the duties of an area studies bibliographer. Although conditions naturally vary from library to library in both countries, I have the impression that the strong financial and bibliographical case for these visits is much more widely acknowledged in the U.S. academic world. For this reason, I feel it doubly important to express my gratitude for the support and encouragement I received from the then Director of the University of London Library, Dr. Donovan Richnell, in the planning and execution of my first, and most wide-ranging, collecting trip.

Because of the limitations imposed by the factors I have described, I aim when planning these visits to try to fit in as many bookshops, agencies and other sources of suitable material as possible, in as many centres as can be reasonably covered within the time and funds at my disposal. I cannot, therefore, be as exhaustive, or as specialized, as I would like; I have very little time to spare for desiderata searching, but have to rely on picking up whatever suitable material is available in each book-shop on the day I visit it.

My first Latin American tour, in 1971, was originally planned to include Brazil, Uruguay, Argentina, Chile, Peru and Mexico, over a period of twelve weeks. In the event, I found it possible to take in Bolivia and Ecuador as well, and the whole journey finally extended to sixteen weeks. I contacted of course all our major suppliers, together with publishers, universities, govern-ment departments, 'cámaras del libro,' and similar trade organiza-tions, since part of my remit was to report to the Committee on Latin American Studies on the booktrade as a whole; but it soon became clear that the most useful aspect of my tour was the opportunity it gave me to visit the less conventional or well-known outlets, particularly the smaller and less library-oriented secondhand dealers. I had taken with me what seemed a more than adequate book fund, but I spent over a third of this in Brazil alone, and additional funds were therefore cabled out to me.

In all, I spent $2,244 on 1,034 items. The final statistics were a clear demonstration of the material benefits of this method of collection-building: The net cost per item, including postage and packing, was $2.25, as against an average cost of $4 for items obtained in the conventional way, whether from Latin American, North American, or U.K. dealers. Even when the cost of travel and accommodation is taken into account, the unit cost per item rises only to $3.25.

On my first trip, I had one major advantage: The Latin American collection then consisted of less than 6,000 volumes, so that the risk of duplication was very low. However, it has now grown to nearly 27,000 volumes, and it will probably not be possible entirely to avoid duplication until a really portable micro-form catalogue of the entire collection is available. Nevertheless, the financial statistics for my 1982 trip were very satisfactory: The average net unit cost was $2.57. If the cost of travel and accommodation is included, this figure rises to $7.68. It must be remembered that this was a very short tour of under two weeks, so that the airfare bulks relatively high as a proportion of the total cost. Even so, this compares very favourably with the figures given in the table of cost statistics for Latin American publications published annually in the SALALM newsletter. The figures given for 1982 in this table indicate an average unit cost for the relevant countries of $8.38.

Since that first major tour I have made two shorter visits, one in 1979 to Puerto Rico, Barbados, Trinidad, Venezuela, Costa Rica, Panama, and Jamaica, and, most recently, in 1982 to Panama, Nicaragua, and Costa Rica. Whatever the length of the tour, however, certain constant features must be borne in mind at the planning stage.

First of all, the tour itself has to be planned as flexibly as possible. Some centres prove much more fruitful than might have been expected; others turn out to be poor sources of material. Preferably, therefore, one should have an open ticket. Flexible ticketing also means that an unexpected public holiday, or a delayed flight, does not provoke a major crisis. It does not seem to be necessary to book hotels in advance, for I have never had any difficulty in finding a room, usually through the booking services provided nowadays at many airports.

Secondly, it is essential to provide for adequate rest periods; travelling and working in tropical or subtropical climates, and in an unfamiliar culture, can be very exhausting. It is dangerously easy to get caught up in the thrill of the chase, and stop for rest only when the bookshops close. Double pneumonia in Paraguay, as happened to one British librarian, is not an experience to be courted.

Thirdly, I have found it better to leave at least half the planned working time spent in any one centre free from formal appointments. If the tour is sponsored in some way by an official body, there is a temptation to agree to a full programme of pre-arranged visits. However, serendipity is the most important factor in this sort of collecting, and it can only be free to operate if one has plenty of time to browse. Although I try also to visit all our regular suppliers, my principal aim is to visit as many as possible of the local book outlets which are not listed in any of the directories, including hotel and airport bookstalls, markets, small stationery stores, department stores, and even the local supermarket.

As soon, therefore, as I have booked into my hotel, I buy a street map and a representative range of local newspapers and periodicals, and try to familiarise myself with the current literary and political climate, significant buzz words, and key names. From the yellow pages I identify useful-looking addresses, and locate them on my map. Wherever possible I try to travel on foot, or at least by public transport, but some cities, like Managua or Caracas, are so extensive and complicated that it is essential to take taxis, or even engage a regular driver. Some taxi-drivers can be a mine of information; my driver in Managua threw himself heart and soul into the task of finding me more bookshops and stalls, and was also invaluable in helping me see my parcels through the post office. Booksellers themselves can often provide useful information about other dealers. In coun-tries where the British Council has a library, the librarian is often a local person, and those I dealt with were very generous with advice as well as moral and material support.

Latin American government publications are not covered in the collection for which I am responsible, since the library of the London School of Economics and the British Library both have extensive holdings of this sort of material. I do not, therefore, normally visit government offices or agencies; and since we have very few exchanges I do not generally visit university departments. But campus bookshops and the publications departments of learned societies can be useful sources of items which are only intended for fairly restricted circulation, such as departmental working papers.

The major practical advantage of these collecting trips, apart from the financial savings I have already described, lie in being able to buy from dealers who do not produce catalogues, and in having the opportunity to negotiate discounts. Even where regular suppliers are concerned, one is able to select from the whole of the dealer's stock, and on the basis of an up-to-date appreciation of the political and cultural context, based on personal experience. On the other hand, very few booksellers or shopkeepers operating on a more modest scale have the capacity to pack the books adequately, much less arrange their export. The expenditure of time and effort, the skilled staff which this process requires, must account for a good proportion of the dealer's markup on catalogue material. Posting packages of books, therefore, is certainly one of the least attractive aspects of this kind of tour.

For a start, anyone setting out on a tour of this kind is advised to pack large quantities of brown paper and string. Brown paper seems to be a very specialized commodity south of the Río Grande, and rarely available, in my experience, from department stores or even stationery shops. Strong string is also difficult to find--I once spent a happy half hour in a large department store in Costa Rica helping the manager unravel a length of thick rope into its constituent strands, so that we could use them to tie up my parcels.

Upon arriving at the post office with neatly packed, securely tied up packages, one may be required to unpack them, and to repack them all over again: They may be over the limits of size or weight acceptable to that particular clerk (standards seem to vary from office to office). In Nicaragua the clerk must have suspected me of attempting to smuggle currency, for she insisted that I unpack all six parcels, and then examined every volume, page by page, before allowing me to repack them. However, in the course of this episode I discovered that quite reasonable string can be bought in the Central Post Office in Managua, although it is apparently not available elsewhere. In Panama, I visited three post offices before finding one that had a weighing machine capable of dealing with parcels; the most helpful and efficient office turned out to be the one located in the former Canal Zone.

It is also useful to take at least one small nylon or string bag of the kind which can be tucked into one's hand-luggage. There always seem to be a few extra volumes picked up in the evening before an early flight or even at the airport itself.

Obviously, the safest way to carry funds is in the form of dollar travellers' cheques, but even here there are pitfalls for the unwary Briton. Sterling cheques are completely unacceptable, and even dollar cheques issued by a British bank are treated with great suspicion. I have also found it wise to carry some cash in dollar bills, so as to be able to take advantage of any 'parallel' or 'grey' currency market. These informal methods of changing money are sometimes legal, sometimes illegal but tolerated, sometimes extremely illegal. The best way to establish if one exists, assuming approaches have not already been made by a member of the hotel staff, seems to be to adopt an innocent expression and ask the porter or maid if they know where it is possible to exchange dollars outside banking hours. The degree of illegality can then be gauged from the style of the response. In one country, where dealings of this sort were definitely illegal, but widely practiced, the porter responded by silently writing the figure 39 on a scrap of paper. This was twice the official rate of exchange.

It might seem safer to have part of one's disposable funds deposited in a local bank to await collection, but this is not without its drawbacks. Some countries will not permit money to be re-exported, even by a visitor, once it has been brought in in this way. It is important, therefore, not to tie up more money than you are likely to spend in that country.

I have been asked on occasion if I have ever had any fears for my personal safety on these tours. On the contrary, in my experience people everywhere are unfailingly kind, helpful, sometimes even overly protective, particularly to the lone traveller. I would like to think that Latin American visitors to the United Kingdom meet with as much courtesy and kindness as I found in their countries.

A much more serious consideration, however, is that the whole enterprise can be, as I have already said, both mentally and physically exhausting. Although these visits are extremely profitable in financial terms, the gain is at the expense of the services for which we pay through the dealer's mark-up. It is difficult to cost in cash terms the experience of an hour spent in a post office queue in tropical heat and humidity. Official procedures in banks and post offices are often complex, obscure, and time-consuming, and coping with them demands linguistic flexibility and emotional resilience. My own fairly brief encounters with these pressures have made me very conscious of the debt we owe to the dealers who regularly face these difficulties on our behalf.

Furthermore, unless one is blessed with adequate support staff in one's home library (and this is, unhappily, seldom the case in British libraries, where often even secretarial staff are lacking), the work of the trip does not come to an end with a return to one's desk. Apart from the follow-up correspondence which is generated, the parcels will soon begin to arrive, at irregular intervals, over a period of up to a year--particularly if the material is coming from the Western countries of Latin America. One of the packages may never arrive at all, or may arrive damaged. The wrapping paper tracked down with such difficulty will have split, the string picked from a length of rope will have broken, and the tattered, waterlogged remains of the treasures will be delivered in a plastic sack, if at all.

There are, however, many compensations which, as far as I am concerned, make every trip well worthwhile. Much of the material obtained in this way is of the kind which, for one reason or another--whether rarity, special interest, age, limited distribution, or lack of commercial appeal--seldom or never appears in a dealer's catalogue. Personal contacts or chance meetings can result in donations, often from the author, of items which are never for sale. Such visits are also often the only effective way to compare and evaluate the commercial and bibliographical performance of the dealers who are already our agents, or whom we are considering using. The sponsoring library saves, of course, a great deal of money. And it is impossible to put any kind of monetary valuation on the increased familiarity with Latin American current events, culture, and patterns of thought which naturally results from such visits, or on the beneficial effects on reference services and future programmes of collection development which this is bound to produce.

14. ACQUISITION FIELD TRIPS TO LATIN AMERICA: AN ANALYSIS

Walter V. Brem, Jr.,

Nelly S. González,

and Heidi Hanson

Acquisition field trips have played an important role in the Latin American collection development process of most libraries. These trips are often undertaken to acquire materials available outside the normal foreign book trade and to establish or review dealer and agency contacts. They are also often costly. Hence, they impinge on both the overall costs of administering a collection and the benefits derived from the additional materials acquired. Thus, an investigation of the role, approach, and results of acquisition field trips in the collection development process should assist libraries in comprehending, assessing, planning, and carrying out future buying trips. The purpose of this paper is to contribute toward this end.

The paper presents and analyzes the results of a questionnaire survey on acquisition field trips to Latin America (Appendix A) sent during May 1984 to 91 SALALM librarians. The survey yielded a response rate of 87 percent. Among those responding, 44 percent had undertaken acquisition field trips, 56 percent had not (table 1).

Table 1

Overall Survey Response

	Number	Percentage
Questionnaires sent	91	
Questionnaires returned	79	87
Respondents having taken field trips	35	44
Respondents not having taken field trips	44	56
	79	100

There is wide variation in the number of trips taken by those who reported having taken trips, from a low of 1 to a high of 12. The frequency distribution is, however, skewed toward the lower end, with approximately 60 percent of the respondents having taken three or fewer trips (table 2).

Table 2

Number of Trips Taken

Number of trips	Number of respondents	Cumulative percentage of respondents
1	10	30
2	3	39
3	7	59
4	5	74
5	2	80
6	3	88
7	1	91
8	1	94
12	2	100
	34*	

*One affirmative response had an undeterminable number of trips.

There is also wide variation in the average amounts spent on purchase of materials per trip (table 3). One respondent reported $0 spent; two respondents reported average expenditures of $20,000 or more. Again, the distribution is skewed toward the lower end of the scale, with 76 percent of the respondents reporting average expenditures of less than $2,000 per trip.

Table 3

Average Amounts Spent per Trip

Average amount spent per trip	Number of respondents	Cumulative percentage of respondents
$ 0 - 499	12	35
$ 500 - 999	9	62
$1,000 - 1,999	5	76
$2,000 - 4,999	3	85
$5,000 - 19,00	3	94
$20,000+	2	100
	34*	

*One affirmative response gave no average amount spent per trip.

Figure 1 (p. 108) shows the relationship between number of trips taken and average amount spent on the purchase of materials per trip. Although only 7 (20 percent) of the 35 respondents having taken trips reported taking 6 trips or more, these respondents account for more than 2/3 of those reporting an average of more than $2,000 per trip spent on materials. It would thus appear that librarians who travel more tend to have greater spending discretion.

In addition, those who take the most trips tend to acquire proportionately fewer volumes free of charge. With two exceptions, all those reporting having acquired over 30 percent of all volumes free of charge took fewer than 6 trips (fig. 2, p. 109).

In sum, analysis of the survey responses shows a positive correlation between the number of trips a particular librarian has taken and the amount spent per trip, and a negative relationship between the number of field trips taken and the percentage of total volumes acquired free of charge.

An acquisition must, by definition, be made either through purchase, exchange, or gift. The survey upon which this analysis is based attempted to measure the percentage of volumes collected in the field that were acquired free of charge and the average amount spent on material purchases. These two variables are plotted for those respondents having made acquisition trips to Latin America on the graph shown in figure 3 (p. 110). The data appear to cluster in three groups. The cluster in the lower right corner describes librarians who spend relatively heavily on materials purchased ($5,000 or more) and acquire a small percentage (20 percent or less) of their materials free of charge. They also tend to be those librarians who make more acquisition field trips. We call them "Aggressive Purchasers" in figure 4 (p. 111), which is a more generalized version of figure 3.

Another cluster, shown in the upper left corner of figure 3, includes librarians who spend relatively little ($500 or less) on an average trip but acquire a high proportion (more than 60 percent) of their volumes free of charge. Their total acquisitions, or number of volumes, could be quite high. They are designated "Gift Maximizers" in figure 4.

A third cluster, shown in the lower left corner of figure 3, perhaps the largest in number, can be characterized as spending relatively little ($2,000 or less) during an acquisition field trip and as acquiring a low proportion (30 percent or less) of volumes free of charge). This group, termed "Low Leverage Acquisitions" in figure 4, tends to make few acquisitions per trip.

The upper right quadrant in figure 4, denominated "Bliss," shows no librarians matching its characteristics in figure 3. This is perhaps because librarians who spend heavily on an average trip would find it difficult to acquire an overall high proportion of volumes free of charge, while those having a high proportion of free acquisitions would very likely see this proportion reduced if they were to spend more heavily.

Figure 1

Number of Trips Taken vs. Average Amount
Spent on Materials Purchased per Trip

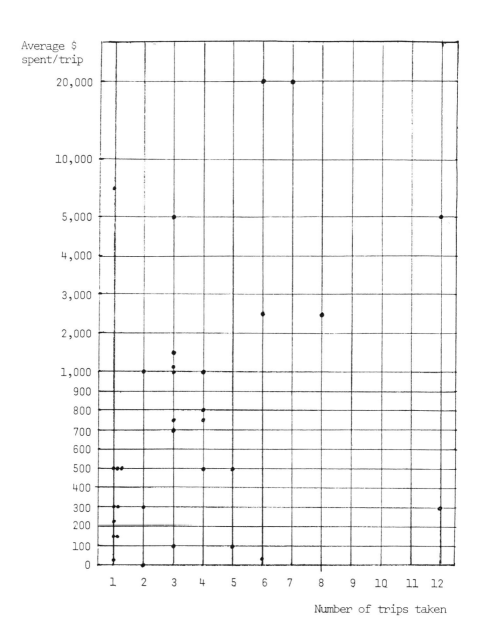

Figure 2

Number of Trips vs. Percentage Gift Acquisition

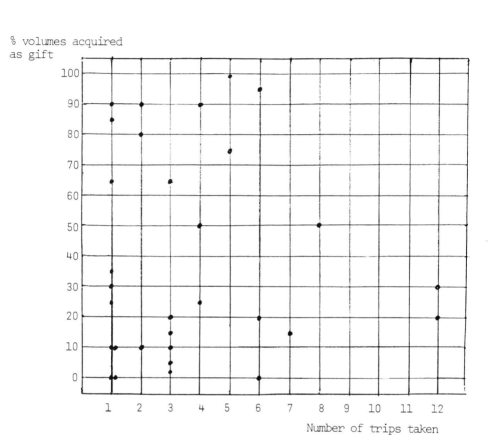

% volumes acquired
as gift

Number of trips taken

Figure 3

Percentage of Volumes Acquired as Gifts vs. Average
Amount Spent on Materials Purchased per Trip

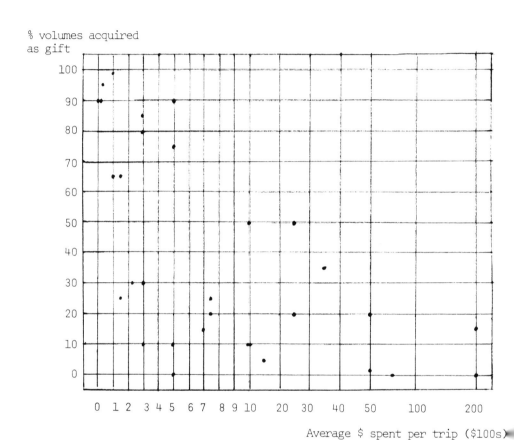

Figure 4

Typology of Foreign Acquisition Field Trip Purchasers

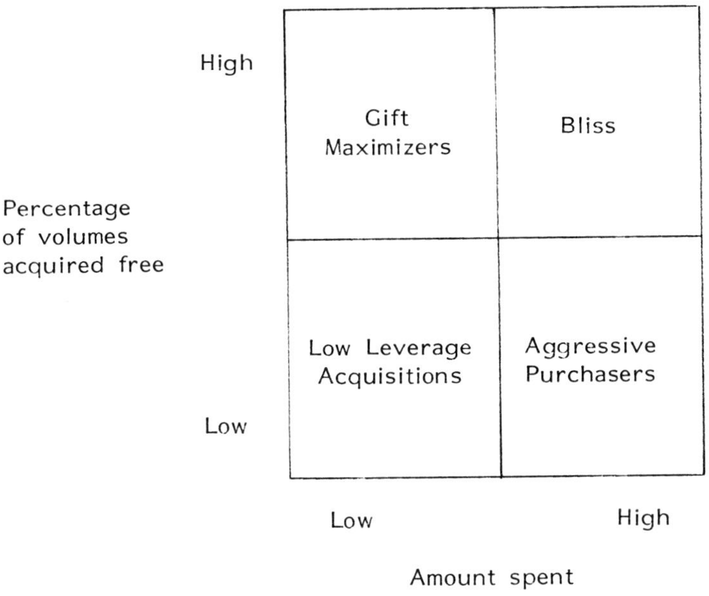

	High	Gift Maximizers	Bliss

Percentage
of volumes
acquired free

	Low Leverage Acquisitions	Aggressive Purchasers

Low

Low   High

Amount spent

Implications

The analysis shows that a substantial proportion of respondents fall into the "Low Leverage Acquisitions" category, which raises questions about the cost-effectiveness of their acquisition field trips. Given the high fixed cost of travel, accommodations, and so on incurred in undertaking a trip to Latin America, it seems appropriate to amortize it over as large a number of volumes acquired as possible, whether through purchase or as gifts or exchanges. This point may be less applicable if the primary purpose of the trip is to establish or renew contacts and not to make acquisitions. For those falling into the "Gift Maximizers" category, it is important to understand the value of materials acquired free of charge relative to those paid for. Finally, it is important to know the determinants of the average amount spent per trip, which has tended to be highest among librarians who have made many trips.

Funding: Type and Source

The vast majority of travel expenses for acquisition trips were fully funded (table 4). Library resources were the principal source of funding for travel, accounting for 47 percent of all trips.

Table 4

Funding Sources for Acquisition Trips

Type of funding for travel	Percentage of trips
Full	65
Transportation only	19
Per diem only	6
None	10
	100

Library Acquisition budgets and reimbursement from Acquisition funds provided 88 percent of the funds used for the purchase of materials. Area Study Centers and Title VI Area Studies funds comprised the remaining 12 percent (table 5, p. 113).

Table 5
Funding Sources for Acquisition Trips

Types of material purchase funding	Percentage of trips
Acquisition funds	59
Personal funds with reimburse- ment from Acquisition funds	24
Endowment funds with reimburse- ment from Acquisition funds	5
Other*	12
	100

*Includes Area Studies Center and Title VI Area Studies funds.

Countries Visited and Types of Materials Sought

The Central American region was visited by the most librarians. Among specific countries, Mexico led, with Peru and Brazil the most immediate followers (table 6).

Table 6
Principal Countries Visited by Librarians on Acquisition Trips

Country or region	Number of visiting librarians
Central America	19*
Mexico	21
Peru	13
Brazil	12
Chile	11
Argentina	11
Colombia	10
Ecuador	8

*Includes those naming "Central America" as a region and those naming one or more individual Central American countries.

When the number of librarians visiting a particular country or region is compared with that country or region's population (a possible measure of an area's importance), a positive correlation results (see fig. 5, p. 114). It is notable, however, that Brazil, with a population of about 130 million, had fewer librarians visiting than did Peru, which has a population less than one-sixth as large, and had almost the same number of reported visits as

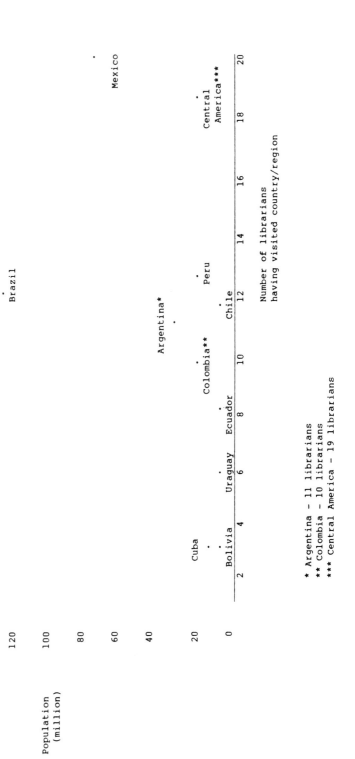

Figure 5

Countries by Population and Number of Visiting Librarians

Colombia and Chile. The high number of librarians visiting Central America may be the result of one or more factors, including the region's recent geopolitical prominence, its proximity to the United States, and the 1983 SALALM meeting held in Costa Rica.

Government documents, serial samples, and maps stood out among the types of materials most sought during field trips to the region (table 7). Government documents featured prominently for all countries. This may be due to the relative abundance of these publications in some countries, such as Brazil, and to the relative unwillingness of book dealers to service government publications. The varying degree of concern for interest group/party publications for various countries, from a high for Central America, Argentina, and Chile to a low for Colombia, may reflect the differing interest in the political issues of these countries and the availability of their publications.

The citing of maps as an area for field trip materials acquisitions was supported by the fact that "Maps" was among the library units most often mentioned as providing direct support for field trips.

Table 7

Total and Percentage of Types of
Materials Sought by Respondents

Country visited	Total visiting	Government documents (national)		Serial samples		Maps		Interest group/party publications	
		no.	%	no.	%	no.	%	no.	%
Argentina	11	10	91	11	100	7	64	6	55
Brazil	12	12	100	9	75	6	50	4	33
Chile	11	10	91	10	91	8	73	6	55
Colombia	10	8	80	6	60	5	50	2	20
Ecuador	8	7	88	6	75	4	50	4	50
Mexico	21	17	81	16	71	8	38	9	43
Peru	13	11	85	10	77	9	69	7	54
Central America	8*	8	100	7	87	5	62	6	75

*Includes only those naming "Central America" as a region.

Operational Issues: Techniques and Resources

Twice as many respondents noted that they write letters to agencies or institutions before departing on a trip as those who do not. About the same proportion report that they believe arriving on the scene without writing ahead of time makes a negative difference in their acquisition results. There seems, however, to be no obvious variable, such as the number of trips taken or amount spent per trip, to explain the difference between those who write before departing and those who do not.

Respondents overwhelmingly supported using the SALALM Newsletter as a clearinghouse of information for librarians embarking on or returning from acquisition field trips. The exact form such a clearinghouse would take is less clear, however: 25 percent of the respondents would be unwilling to publish summaries of their trips and less than half would be able and willing to buy multiple copies of difficult-to-get materials for other libraries. This relative unwillingness was particularly high among librarians having made five or more acquisition field trips.

Summary and Conclusions

Acquisition field trips play an important role in the acquisition of materials available outside the normal foreign book trade, establishment and renewal of dealer and agency contacts, and learning or updating knowledge of trends in the book trade. Nonetheless, institutions vary in the importance they place on these trips. Slightly less than half of the librarians who responded to the survey had ever taken a field trip. Among those taking trips, the number of trips varied widely, but 59 percent had taken between one and three trips.

The relatively small number of respondents who have taken trips tend to spend the largest amount per trip on materials. Interestingly, a cluster analysis of data comparing the attributes of amount spent per trip and percentage of materials acquired free of charge showed three groupings:

> Those spending relatively little but acquiring a high
> proportion of volumes free of charge, often over
> 80 percent
> Those spending relatively heavily but acquiring a low
> proportion of volumes free of charge, tending to be
> the more traveled librarians
> Those spending relatively little and acquiring a low
> proportion of volumes free of charge.

The largest number of librarians visited Mexico, 21 having undertaken fieldwork there. Central America was next, with 19, followed by Peru and Brazil. Government documents and serial samples were the most sought after materials (see Appendix B).

This investigation is an initial undertaking toward creating a better understanding of the role of acquisition field trips in the collection development process. It has raised many issues which subsequent research must answer. Nonetheless, it should assist librarians in comprehending, assessing, planning, and carrying out field trips to Latin America and the Caribbean.

Appendix A
Acquisition Field Trips
A SALALM Survey

INTRODUCTION

1. Do you make acquisition field trips?   yes ___   no ___

   If you have not made any field trips you need not complete the remainder of the questionnaire; please return it as soon as possible.

2. Title: please mark the title that describes your position.

   ___ Bibliographer   ___ Gift and Exchange librarian
   ___ Reference librarian/subject specialist ___ Acquisition librarian
   ___ Reference librarian   ___ Other (specify) _____

ADMINISTRATIVE AND FINANCIAL SUPPORT

3. Funding for travel: please indicate the number of trips taken at full funding, partial-funding, or no funding.

   ___ Full funding   ___ Partial funding: Per diem
   ___ Partial funding: transportation   ___ No funding

4. Sources of funding for travel: please indicate the number of trips taken using the types of funding listed below.

   ___ Library   ___ University or Institutional
   ___ Latin American Area Studies Center   Administration
   ___ Joint Library/Area Studies Center/   ___ Endowment funds
       University Administration   ___ Other funds (please specify)
                                              _____

COLLECTION AND ACQUSITION ACTIVITIES

5. Funding for purchases of materials: please indicate the types of funding used for on-site purchases.

   ___ Acquisitions funds   ___ Personal funds with reimbursement
   ___ Endowment funds with reimbursement   from Acquisitions funds
       from Acquisitions funds   ___ Other funds (please specify)
                                              _____

6. Please estimate the average amount you spend on materials purchases for each trip $_____

7. Of all volumes collected in the field, on average, please estimate what percentage were acquired free? _____%

7A. On an average, what is the duration of your field trips?

8. The next question asks for information about 1) the countries or regions to which you make field trips, and 2) the types of materials sought for each country or region.

Please list the countries and/or regions visited in the left-hand column of the table below, and indicate the category of materials sought by marking the appropriate column(s) under each category. Please be specific: If the materials sought for an individual country within a region (e.g., the Caribbean) differ significantly from the materials sought for that region as a whole, please list that country separately. (Several examples have been given as a guide.)

COUNTRY OR REGION	Current monographs	Out-of-print monographs	Serial samples	Serial backfiles (complete / fill ins)	Govt. documents: National	Govt. documents: Provincial/state	Govt. documents: Local	Learned society publications	Maps	Personal libraries; dealer-assembled collections	Professional assn./ labor organization publications	Interest/pressure group, party publ.	Other (specify):
Examples:													
Brazil		✓			✓	✓					✓	✓	
Central America	✓	✓			✓		✓		✓			·	
Mexico		✓	✓	✓	✓	✓		✓		✓		✓	✓

8A. Briefly, please itemize the reasons why you travel to acquire the kinds of materials checked off in the grid on the previous page. (Please continue on the last page, if necessary).

_____

_____

_____

_____

OTHER INSTITUTIONAL ACTIVITIES

On field trips it is assumed that librarians advance their current awareness of publishing and the book trades, maintain and develop contacts with a wide variety of persons and institutions, clarify profiles or procedures with book vendors or gifts and exchange partners, and sometimes rescue materials and clear snags for purchased materials not shipped by institutions or vendors, but there may be a variety of activities in support of technical and public service units that are unrecognized. The following two questions seek to identify some of those activities.

9. Do you carry out any activities in direct support of other library units?

___ yes   ___ no

If "yes", please specify the units and the type of activity you have done.

_____

_____

_____

_____

10. Do you see any public service or reference uses in your field trips?

___ yes   ___ no

If "yes", please describe. _____

_____

_____

_____

TECHNIQUES AND RESOURCES

11. Do you write letters to agencies or institutes before departing on a trip?

___ yes   ___ no

12. Do you think arriving on the scene without writing ahead of time makes a difference in the results of acquiring materials?

___ yes   ___ no

13. In what specific situations has writing prior to departure been the most beneficial in acquiring materials?

_____

_____

_____

_____

14. Do you take desiderata lists on your trips?   ___ yes   ___ no

15. If "yes", what kind of materials do you include on your lists? _____

_____

_____

16. Do you take your own packing supplies? ___ yes   ___ no   If "yes", what do you take? _____

_____

17. Do you ship materials through vendors and the mails only?   ___ yes   ___ no
If "no", what other means do you use? _____

18. Do you use embassy, consular, or chamber of commerce offices in making contacts, developing or updating information?   ___ yes   ___ no
If "yes", what kinds of information do you find useful? _____

_____

_____

19. To identify sources of materials, such as research centers, institutes, government agencies, small publishers, and so forth, have you found any recently published handbooks, bibliographies, or directories (in addition to the telephone directories), etc., that you have found especially helpful? Please list below the most significant or useful sources from any region or country.

_____

_____

_____

_____

_____

_____

_____

_____

_____

NETWORKING

20. Do you think the SALALM Newsletter should be used as a clearinghouse of information for librarians embarking on or returning from acquisition field trips?

____ yes   ____ no

21. Would you be willing to publish a summary of your trips in the SALALM Newsletter?

____ yes   ____ no

22. Are you willing to share unpublished travel reports with librarians planning to travel to an area or country where you have been?

____ yes   ____ no

23. Are you able and willing to buy multiple copies of difficult-to-get materials for other libraries?

____ yes   ____ no

24. Comments, elaboration, suggestions, etc.

Appendix B
Summary of Responses
Number of Trips and Materials Acquired by Country or Region

	COUNTRY OR REGION	CURRENT MONOGRAPHS	OUT-OF-PRINT MONOGRAPHS	SERIAL SAMPLES	SERIAL BACKFILES (complete/fill ins)	GOVT. DOCUMENTS: NATIONAL	GOVT. DOCUMENTS: PROVINCIAL/STATE	GOVT. DOCUMENTS: LOCAL	LEARNED SOCIETY PUBLICATIONS AND RESEARCH CENTERS	MAPS	PERSONAL LIBRARIES DEALER-ASSEMBLED COLLECTIONS	PROFESSIONAL ASSN./LABOR ORG. PUB.	INTEREST/PRESSURE GROUP, PARTY PUBL.	OTHER (SPECIFY)
21	Mexico	9	7	16	11	17	8	6	13	8	3	10	9	1 AV Materials
13	Peru	13	7	10	10	11	11	4	7	9	5	5	7	1 Hist. Photog.
12	Brazil	6	7	9	7	12	10	9	8	6	4	6	4	1 Miscellaneous
11	Chile	7	6	10	7	10	2	2	6	8	2	4	6	1 Miscellaneous
11	Argentina	7	5	11	5	10	3	3	9	7	5	6	6	0
10	Colombia	6	4	6	6	8	3	2	9	5	3	4	2	3 Miscellaneous
8	Ecuador	5	5	6	6	7	2	1	4	4	2	2	4	3 Miscellaneous
5	Venezuela	4	3	5	3	5	2	2	5	2	1	4	2	1 Miscellaneous
4	Paraguay	4	4	4	2	4	2	0	2	2	0	2	2	2 Miscellaneous
3	Bolivia	1	2	2	1	3	1	0	0	2	0	0	0	0
8	Central America	7	3	7	3	8	4	3	8	5	2	6	6	4 Miscellaneous
15	Costa Rica	8	1	7	4	8	0	0	5	2	0	2	2	1 Miscellaneous
11	Nicaragua	12	4	12	10	12	2	2	9	9	2	4	9	1 AV Materials
4	Honduras	2	0	4	2	4	0	0	4	0	0	2	0	1 Miscellaneous
5	Panama	4	3	3	3	4	3	2	3	2	1	2	2	2 Miscellaneous
2	Guatemala	2	0	2	1	2	1	1	2	1	0	1	1	0
3	Caribbean	3	2	3	3	3	3	1	3	3	0	3	3	0
5	Cuba	4	2	4	3	5	4	2	1	6	0	0	0	0
2	Puerto Rico	2	0	2	0	2	0	0	2	0	0	2	0	1 Miscellaneous
2	Dominican Republic	2	0	2	0	2	0	0	2	0	0	2	0	1 Miscellaneous
3	Jamaica	3	0	2	0	3	0	0	2	0	0	2	0	1 Miscellaneous
3	Netherlands Antilles	0	0	2	0	2	0	2	2	0	0	2	0	1 Miscellaneous
6	Uruguay	4	3	5	3	5	1	0	3	2	1	1	1	0
2	Portugal	1	1	2	1	2	0	0	2	0	1	0	1	0
2	Spain	1	1	2	2	2	2	2	2	1	1	2	2	0
1	Trinidad	1	0	0	0	1	0	0	0	0	0	0	0	0
1	South America	0	0	1	0	1	0	0	1	0	0	1	1	1 AV Materials

Bibliographies and Reference Aids

15. LIBRARY RESOURCES IN LATIN AMERICA AND THE
CARIBBEAN: BIBLIOGRAPHY OF GUIDES AND DIRECTORIES
OF LATIN AMERICAN AND CARIBBEAN LIBRARIES,
ARCHIVES AND INFORMATION CENTERS

Celia Leyte-Vidal and Jesús Leyte-Vidal

Introduction

This bibliography was compiled to focus attention on information resources in Latin America and the Caribbean. In assembling the list we relied on the OCLC Online Union Catalog, the Library of Congress's Subject Catalog, and Professor William V. Jackson's Directories of Latin American Libraries. A preliminary version of this work was published in the Papers of SALALM XXVII;* items that appeared there are preceded by an asterisk (*). This final version is the result of the combined efforts of the following members of the Ad Hoc Subcommittee on Compiling Directories of Latin American Libraries: Aurelio Alvarez y Juan, Elsa Barberena, Cecilia Culebra Vives, Nelly González, and Thomas L. Welch.

The bibliography is arranged alphabetically by country and by author or title within each country. Guides treating more than two countries are listed first, under the heading "General." The entries are numbered consecutively. The hyphenated number immediately after the entry is the Library of Congress card number. The following number, if any, is the OCLC number. This information is included to aid retrieval of the records. The initials in parentheses following some entries indicate the source of the citation: Professor Jackson's list (WVJ) or one of the collaborators named above.

Inconsistencies may exist in this work, as we have made no effort to verify or correct the entries. They are listed more or less as they appear in the bibliographic tools consulted or as contributed, although an effort has been made to standardize the format of the entries. In order to be as thorough as possible, we have in some cases recorded various editions of the same title.

---

*Public Policy Issues and Latin American Library Resources: Papers of the Seminar on the Acquisition of Latin American Library Materials XXVII, Washington, DC, March 2-5, 1982. (Madison, WI: SALALM, 1984), pp. 221-232.

General

* 1. Asociación Latinoamericana de Instituciones Financieras de
       Desarrollo. Directorio de unidades de información en las
       Instituciones miembros del ALIDE. Lima: La Asociación,
       1979 or 1980. 70 leaves. LC 80-128625.

   2. Association of Caribbean Universities and Research Insti-
       tutes. Directory of Caribbean Research Institutes /
       Directorios de centros de investigación del Caribe.
       [Kingston]:   The   Association,   [19--].   55 leaves.
       LC 76-379672.

* 3. Columbus Memorial Library. Guía de bibliotecas de la Amé-
       rica Latina. Bibliographic Series, 51. Washington, DC:
       Unión Panamericana, 1963. viii, 165 pp. LC pa63-12/r81.

   4. Directorio de servicios de información sobre formación pro-
       fesional de América Latina. Montevideo: CINTERFOR/
       OIT, 1981. 126 pp. LC 82-141410.

   5. Directory of Adult Education Documentation and Information
       Services / Repertorio de servicios de documentación e
       información sobre educación de adultos. 2d ed. IBEDATA
       Reference Series. Paris: UNESCO, 1980. 112 pp.
       LC 80-515456/r81.

   6. Directory of Educational Documentation and Information
       Services / Repertoire des services de documentation et
       d'information pedagogiques. IBEDOC Reference Series.
       Paris: UNESCO. Vol. 1--. 1975--. LC 77-648879.

   7. Directory of Educational Documentation and Information
       Services / Repertoire des services de documentation et
       d'information pedagogiques. 3rd ed. IBEDATA Reference
       Series. Paris: UNESCO. 1979--. LC sn82-20497.

   8. Directory of World Bank Depository Libraries. [s.i.: s.n.,
       1983?]. (NG)

   9. Garst, Rachel. "Guide to the Major Libraries of Central
       America." In Bibliografía anotada de obras de referencia
       sobre Centroamérica y Panamá en el campo de las ciencias
       sociales. 2 vols. San José: Instituto de Investigaciones
       Sociales, Universidad de Costa Rica, [1983?].

  10. Hernández de Caldas, Angela. Bibliotecas y centros de
       documentación bio-agrícolas latinoamericanos. Bogotá:
       [Ministerio de Educación Nacional, Sección de Servicios
       Bibliotecarios], 1968. 10 leaves. LC 78-414921.

  11. International Library Directory. London: A. P. Wales
       Organization, Pub. Division. Vol. 1--. 1963--. (TLW)

* 12. Jefferson, Albertina A., and Alvona Alleyne. "Caribbeana Resources in the English-speaking Caribbean. Final Report and Working Papers of the Twenty-Fourth Seminar on the Acquisition of Latin American Library Materials. Los Angeles, CA, June 17-22, 1979. Madison, WI: SALALM, 1980. Pp. 263-286.

13. Lewanski, Richard Casimir. Library Directories: Library Science Dictionaries. Bibliography and Reference Series, 4. Santa Barbara, CA: [American Bibliographical Center], 1967. 40 pp. (TLW)

14. Nauman, Ann Keith. A Handbook of Latin American and Caribbean National Archives / Guía de los archivos nacionales de América Latina y el Caribe. Detroit, MI: Blaine Ethridge, 1983. ix, 127 pp. LC 83-15837.

* 15. Oliveira, Regina Maria Soares de. Guia dos usuários da Classificação Decimal Universal (CDU) na América Latina: bibliotecas, centros e serviços de documentação / Directory of Universal Decimal Classification (UDC) Users in Latin America: Libraries and Documentation-Information Centres and Services. FID publication, 558. Rio de Janeiro: Conselho Nacional de Desenvolvimento Científico e Tecnológico, Instituto Brasileiro de Informação em Ciência e Tecnologia, 1977. 151 pp. LC 79-119486.

16. Peraza Sarauza, Fermín. Las bibliotecas de México, Guatemala, El Salvador y Honduras; notas de viaje. Havana: Anuario Bibliográfico Cubano, 1946. 35 pp. (TLW)

17. _____. Las bibliotecas del Caribe. Havana: Anuario Bibliográfico Cubano, 1943. 40 pp. (TLW)

* 18. Research Guide to Andean History: Bolivia, Chile, Ecuador and Peru. Contributing eds., Judith R. Bakewell et al. Coordinating ed., John J. TePaske. Durham, NC: Duke University Press, 1981. xiii, 346 pp. LC 80-29365.

19. Steele, Colin. Major Libraries of the World: A Selective Guide. London and New York, NY: Bowker, 1976. xix, 479 pp. LC 77-369002.

20. World Directory of Social Science Institutions / Repertorio mundial de instituciones de ciencias sociales. 2d ed., rev. World Social Science Information Services, 2. [Paris]: UNESCO Social Science Documentation Centre, 1979. xvi, 485 pp. LC 81-459410.

21. World Directory of Social Science Institutions / Repertorio mundial de instituciones de ciencias sociales. 3d ed., rev. World Social Science Information Services, 2. Paris: UNESCO, 1982. 535 pp. OCLC 9176254.

* 22. World Guide to Libraries / Internationales Bibliotheks-
      Handbuch. 3d ed. 4 vols. New York, NY: Bowker;
      Pullach/Munich: Verlag Dokumentation, 1970. OCLC
      1211667.

  23. World Guide to Libraries / Internationales Bibliotheks-
      Handbuch. 4th ed. 2 vols. New York, NY: Bowker;
      Pullach/Munich: Verlag Dokumentation, 1974. OCLC
      1005009.

* 24. World Guide to Libraries / Internationales Bibliotheks-
      Handbuch. H. Lengenfelder, ed. 5th ed. Handbook of
      International Documentation and Information, 8. New
      York, NY: Saur, 1980. xxv, 1030 pp. OCLC 6592292.

  25. World Guide to Science Information and Documentation Ser-
      vices / Guide mondial des centres de documentation et
      d'information scientifiques. Documentation and Termi-
      nology of Science. Paris: UNESCO, 1965. 211 pp.
      LC 65-9614.

  26. World Guide to Technical Information and Documentation
      Services / Guide mondial des centres de documentation et
      d'information techniques. [Paris: UNESCO, 1969.]
      287 pp. LC 72-16838.

  27. World Guide to Technical Information and Documentation
      Services / Guide mondial des centres de documentation et
      d'information techniques. 2d ed. rev. and enl. Docu-
      mentation, Libraries, and Archives: Bibliographies and
      Reference Works, 2. Paris: UNESCO, 1975. 515 pp.
      LC 75-325752.

Argentina

  28. Argentina. Comisión protectora de Bibliotecas Populares.
      Nómina de las bibliotecas populares protegidas. Buenos
      Aires: 1947. 71 pp. (TLW)

* 29. Bahía Blanca, Argentina. Universidad Nacional del Sur.
      Centro de Documentación Bibliotecológica. Guía: Biblio-
      tecas universitarias argentinas. Bahía Blanca: 1967.
      (WVJ)

* 30. _____. Guía de las bibliotecas universitarias argen-
      tinas. 3d ed. Buenos Aires: Casa Pardo, 1976.
      207 pp. LC 77-568272.

* 31. Deransart, Pierre. Bibliotheques et systemes documentaires
      en Argentine et au Bresil. Le Chasnay: Institut de
      recherche d'informatique et d'automatique, [1977?]
      145 pp. LC 78-363138.

* 32. Giuffra, Carlos Alberto. Guía de bibliotecas argentinas.
       Edición preliminar. Buenos Aires: Fundación Inter-
       americana de Bibliotecología Franklin y Comisión Nacional
       Argentina para UNESCO, 1967. 334 pp. LC 68-111377.

* 33. Guía de las bibliotecas universitarias argentinas. Univer-
       sidad Nacional del Sur, Centro de Investigaciones Biblio-
       tecológicas. Buenos Aires: Casa Pardo, 1976. 107 pp.
       OCLC 3050560.

* 34. Matijevic, Nicolás. Guía: bibliotecas universitarias
       argentinas. Bahía Blanca: Centro de Documentación
       Bibliotecológica, Universidad Nacional del Sur. 1967. iii,
       166 pp. LC 68-90856.

  35. _____ . Guía de las bibliotecas universitarias
       argentinas. Bahía Blanca: Centro de Documentación
       Bibliotecológica, Universidad del Sur, 1970. 181 leaves.
       LC 75-856468.

* 36. _____ . Guía de las bibliotecas universitarias
       argentinas. Bahía Blanca: Centro de Documentación
       Bibliotecológica, Universidad del Sur, 1970. 43 leaves.
       LC 75-28756/7-82.

* 37. _____ . Guía de las bibliotecas universitarias argen-
       tinas. Buenos Aires: Casa Pardo, Centro de Documenta-
       ción Bibliotecológica, 1976. 181 leaves. OCLC 3029350.

* 38. Río Negro, Argentina. Dirección Provincial de Cultura.
       Departamento de Bibliotecas. Guía de bibliotecas de
       Río Negro. Publicaciones generales del Consejo Provincial
       de Educación, 4. Viedma: Consejo Provincial de Educa-
       ción, 1973. 57 pp. OCLC 5123563.

* 39. Universidad de Buenos Aires. Instituto Bibliotecológico.
       Guía de las bibliotecas de la Universidad de Buenos
       Aires. Buenos Aires: 1962. 51 pp. OCLC 1651144.

* 40. _____ . Guía de las bibliotecas de la Universidad
       de Buenos Aires. 2d ed. Buenos Aires: 1966. 64 pp.
       LC 70-238241.

* 41. _____ . Guía de las bibliotecas de la Universidad
       de Buenos Aires. 3d ed. Buenos Aires: 1970. 87 pp.
       LC 71-275791.

Bolivia

* 42. Centro Nacional de Documentación Científica y Tecnológica.
       Guía de bibliotecas, centros y servicios documentarios de
       Bolivia, 1973. La Paz: Universidad Mayor de San
       Andrés, 1973. 113 pp. OCLC 1200070.

* 43. Directorio de bibliotecas y centros de documentación de
       Bolivia, 1978. Publicación 1. La Paz: SYFNID, 1978.
       109 pp. OCLC 6989600.

Brazil

* 44. Associação Paulista de Bibliotecários. Grupo de Trabalho em
       Bibliotecas de Ciências Sociais e Humanas. Guia de
       bibliotecas de Ciências sociais e humanas do Estado de São
       Paulo. Ed. preliminar. São Paulo: 1973. 44 leaves.
       LC 75-574951/r76.

  45. Associação Profissional de Bibliotecários de Pernambuco.
       Guia das bibliotecas e bibliotecários do Recife. 2d ed.,
       rev. e aumentada. Recife: 1971. 120 pp. (TLW)

  46. Associação Profissional dos Bibliotecários do Estado do Rio de
       Janeiro. Grupo de Bibliotecários em Informação e
       Documentação Agrícola. Directorio de bibliotecas em
       ciências agrícolas do Rio de Janeiro. Rio de Janeiro:
       O Grupo, 1979. 47 leaves. OCLC 650485.

  47. Bettiol, O., and F. B. Margalho. Guia das bibliotecas
       de ciências agrarias, ensino superior. 2d ed., rev.
       e ampliada. Brasília: Ministerio da Educação e
       Cultura, Secretaria de Ensino Superior, 1982. 134 pp.
       LC 82-246794.

* 48. Brazil. Instituto Nacional do Livro. Guia das bibliotecas
       brasileiras. 4th ed. Rio de Janeiro: 1969. (WVJ)

* 49. Comissão Brasileira de Classificação Decimal Universal.
       Levantamento dos usuarios da CDU no Brasil. Publicação
       avulsa, IBBD/CDU, 1. Rio de Janeiro: O instituto,
       1975. 34 leaves. LC 78-383433.

  50. Costa, Humberto Soares da. Bibliotecas do centro-oeste do
       Brasil. Coleção B2: Biblioteconomia, 9. Ministerio da
       Educação e Cultura. Instituto Nacional do Livro, 1953.
       130 pp. (TLW)

* 51. Fundação Instituto Brasileiro de Geografia e Estatística.
       Guia das bibliotecas brasileiras, 1976. Rio de Janeiro:
       Fundação Instituto Brasileiro de Geografia e Estatística,
       Instituto Nacional do Livro, 1979. 11, 1017 pp.
       OCLC 6588118.

* 52. Guias das bibliotecas brasileiras. Rio de Janeiro: Secretaria
       de Planejamento da Presidência da Republica. Fundação
       Instituto Brasileiro de Geografia e Estatística, Directoria
       Técnica. 1941--. LC 80-646415.

  53. Guia das bibliotecas de Brasília, 1975. [Trabalho elaborado
       por Conselho Regional de Biblioteconomia, Ia. Região,
       Departamento de Biblioteconomia da Universidade de

Brasília, Associação dos Bibliotecários do Distrito Federal]. Brasília: Ediciones ABDF, 1975. 52 pp. OCLC 2552329.

* 54. Guia das bibliotecas do Estado de Minas Gerais. Belo Horizonte: Conselho de Extensão da UFMG. Vols. for 1977-- issued by the Conselho Regional de Biblioteconomia, 6a. Região. 1977--. LC 78-646033.

* 55. Guia das bibliotecas do Estado de São Paulo. São Paulo: Secretaria de Cultura, Ciência e Tecnologia do Estado de São Paulo, Departamento de Artes e Ciências Humanas, Divisão de Bibliotecas. 1978--. LC 79-645196.

* 56. Guia de bibliotecas universitarias brasileiras. Brasília: Ministerio de Educação e Cultura, Departamento de Assuntos Universitarios, Coordenação do Aperfeiçoamento de Pessoal de Nivel Superior. 1979--. LC 80-642703.

57. Pereira, Maria de Nazaré Freitas. A rede de bibliotecas da Amazônia. Belém: Ministerio do Interior, Superintendência do Desenvolvimento da Amazônia, Assessoria de Programação e Coordenação, Divisão de Documentação, 1973. 14, [32] pp. LC 75-541992.

58. Pernambuco, Brazil (State). Universidade Federal. Biblioteca Central. Guia das bibliotecas da Universidade Federal de Pernambuco. Comp. Ida Brandão de São Pessoa. 2d ed. Recife: 1969. LC 72-219942.

* 59. Rio de Janeiro. Instituto Nacional do Livro. Guia das bibliotecas brasileiras. Coleção B2, Biblioteconomia, 2. Rio de Janeiro: 1941. 245 pp. LC 41-15980.

* 60. _____. Guia das bibliotecas brasileiras, registadas até 31 de março de 1942. 2d ed. Coleção B2, Biblioteconomia, 2. Rio de Janeiro: Imprensa nacional, 1944. 475 pp. LC 46-1902.

* 61. _____. Guia das bibliotecas brasileiras, registradas até 31 de dezembro de 1952. 3d ed. Rio de Janeiro: 1955. 678 pp. LC 56-25294.

* 62. _____. Guia das bibliotecas brasileiras referente a 31 de dezembro de 1965. Informe especial para o V Congresso Brasileiro de Biblioteconomia e Documentação a realizarse em São Paulo de 8 a 15 de janeiro de 1967. Rio de Janeiro: 1967. 21 pp. OCLC 3652685.

63. Rocha, M. L. B. P. de, and E. P. de Sant'Anna. Guia das bibliotecas. Salvador: Universidade Federal da Bahia, Biblioteca Central, 1971. 82 pp. OCLC 1019262.

64. São Paulo, Brazil (City). Universidade. Biblioteca Central. Guia das bibliotecas da Universidade de São Paulo. [São Paulo]: A Biblioteca, 1973. xii, 110 pp. LC 77-575269.

* 65. Seckinger, Ron, and F. W. O. Morton. "Social Science Libraries in Greater Rio de Janeiro." Latin American Research Review, 14 (1979), 180-201. (WVJ)

* 66. Tavares, Maria Teresa Wiltgen. Bibliotecas no Rio Grande do Sul, 1971-1972. Porto Alegre: Governo do Estado do Rio Grande do Sul, Secretaria de Coordinação e Planejamento Global, 1973. 84 pp. LC 79-350170.

* 67. Uratsuka, Josefa Naoco. Guia de bibliotecas de ciências sociais e humanas do Estado de São Paulo. São Paulo: Associação Paulista de Bibliotecários, Grupo de Trabalho em Bibliotecas de Ciências Sociais e Humanas, 1974. 61 leaves. LC 76-460873.

Chile

68. Chile. Guía de bibliotecas y centros de documentación de Chile. Ser. Directorios, 1. Santiago: Centro Nacional de Información y Documentación, 1972. iii, 120 pp. OCLC 4367012.

69. _____. Guía de bibliotecas especializadas y centros de documentación de Chile. 2d ed. Ser. Directorios, 2. Santiago: Dirección de Información y Documentación, 1976. (WVJ)

70. Sehlinger, Peter J. A Select Guide to Chilean Libraries and Archives. Latin American Studies Working Papers, 9. Bloomington, IN: Latin American Studies Program, Indiana University, 1979. 35 pp. LC 80-108172.

71. Silva Castro, Raul. Biblioteca nacional y biblioteca pública. Ediciones Instante, 23. [Angol, Malleco (Chile): Impr. Index, 1950?] 33 pp. (TLW)

72. United Nations. Economic Commission for Latin America. Directorio de unidades de información para el desarrollo: Chile. Santiago de Chile: CEPAL, 1978. vii, 203 pp. LC 79-110307.

73. Universidad de Chile. Vicerrectoría de Extensión y Comunicaciones. Guía de Bibliotecas. Santiago: Ediciones de la Universidad de Chile, 1980. 74, [1] pp. OCLC 7527653.

Colombia

74. Cali, Colombia. Universidad del Valle. Facultad de Arquitectura. Guía de las bibliotecas y centros de investigación de Cali. Ed. preliminar. Cali: 1961. 30 pp. LC 76-86342.

75. Colombia. Departamento Administrativo Nacional de Estadística. La Biblioteca en Colombia, 1964. 5th ed. Bogotá: 1966. (WVJ)

76. Directorio colombiano de unidades de información. Serie Información y documentación. Bogotá: Imprenta Nacional, 1976--. LC 78-641315.

77. Directorio unidades de información ciencias del mar. Bogotá: Fondo Colombiano de Investigaciones Científicas y Proyectos Especiales Francisco José de Caldas Colciencias, 1981. 117 pp. OCLC 9138637.

78. Florén Lozano, L., and J. Castañeda. Guía de las bibliotecas de Medellín. Medellín: Editorial Universitaria de Antioquía, 1966. 136 pp. LC 68-11381.

79. Guía de las bibliotecas de Medellín. Ed. provisional. Medellín: Escuela Interamericana de Bibliotecología, 1961. 15 pp. OCLC 8325060.

80. Instituto Colombiano de Cultura. Directorio colombiano de bibliotecas públicas/Instituto Colombiano de Cultura. Biblioteca para el desarrollo cultural, 1. [Bogotá: Instituto Colombiano de Cultura, Subdirección de Communicaciones Culturales, División de Desarrollo Cultural de la Comunidad, Sección de Bibliotecas, 1977.] 81 pp. (TLW)

* 81. Programa Interinstitucional de Documentación. Directorio de recursos bibliográficos del Valle de Aburra. Medellín: Programa Interinstitucional de Documentación, 1975. 22, 53 pp. LC 79-128949.

* 82. Rojas L., O. G., and A. Salazar Alonso. Directorio colombiano de bibliotecas y centros de información y documentación. Serie Directorios y repertorios, Colciencias, 2. Bogotá: Colciencias, División de Documentación, 1973. vii, 187 leaves. LC 80-144458.

Costa Rica

* 83. Consejo Nacional de Investigaciones Científicas y Tecnológicas, Costa Rica. Guía de bibliotecas, archivos, servicios y centros de información y documentación en Costa Rica. San José: Departamento de Información y Documentación, CONICYIT, 1975. (WVJ)

Cuba

* 84. Directorio de bibliotecas de Cuba. Comp. Fermín Peraza Sarausa. Biblioteca del bibliotecario, 2. Gainesville, FL; Havana: Anuario Bibliográfico Cubano. 1942--. Publication suspended 1953-1962. LC 44-35650.

* 85. Guía de bibliotecas de la República de Cuba. Havana:
       Biblioteca Nacional "José Martí." 1976--. LC 76-235490.

* 86. Havana. Biblioteca Nacional José Martí. Departamento
       Metódio. Guía de bibliotecas de la República de Cuba.
       2d rev. ed. Havana: 1966. 107 pp.

* 87. _____. Departamento de Información de Ciencia y
       Técnica. Guía de bibliotecas y centros de documentación
       de la República de Cuba. 3d ed. Havana: 1970.
       101 pp. OCLC 729307.

  88. Peraza Sarauza, Fermín. Bibliotecas universitarias, su
       actual origen con especial referencia a las bibliotecas
       universitarias cubanas. Santa Clara: 1955. 29 pp.
       (TLW)

Ecuador

* 89. Centro Latinoamericano de Documentación Económica y
       Social. Directorio de unidades de información para el
       desarrollo: Ecuador. Santiago: El Centro, 1978. 52 pp.
       OCLC 5530130.

* 90. Preibish, Andre. Directorio/Guía de las bibliotecas en
       Ecuador. Ottawa: National Library of Canada, Collection
       Development Branch, 1979. vii, 117 pp. OCLC 6883915.

Guatemala

  91. Directorio de unidades de información para el desarrollo,
       Guatemala. Santiago: Centro Latinoamericano de Docu-
       mentación Económica y Social, Comisión Económica para
       América Latina, 1979. vii, 64 pp. LC 82-232769.

Guyana

* 92. Stephenson, Yvonne. A Guide to Library Services in
       Guyana. Georgetown: Guyana Library Association,
       1972. (WVJ)

Jamaica

* 93. Jamaica. National Council on Libraries, Archives and Docu-
       mentation Services. Directory of Information Resources in
       Jamaica. Kingston: 1977. (WVJ)

* 94. Richards, Judith E. Directory of Jamaican Libraries.
       Kingston: Jamaica Library Association, 1967--.
       LC 76-367049.

Mexico

* 95. Barberena B., Elsa. Directorio de bibliotecas de la Ciudad
       de México / Directory of Mexico City Libraries. 2d rev.
       ed. México, DF: University of the Americas, 1967.
       xxii, 259 pp. LC 79-207319.

  96. Block Iturriaga, Carmen. Unidades de información en el
       area científica en México. Cuadernos de ABIESI, 12.
       México, DF: Asociación de Bibliotecarios de Instituciones
       de Enseñanza Superior e Investigaciones, 1982.
       [72 pp.]   (EB)

  97. Consejo Nacional de Ciencia y Tecnología. Directorio de
       fuentes y recursos para la información documental.
       Serie Directorios y Catálogos, 5. México, DF: Consejo
       Nacional de Ciencia y Tecnología, 1978. xi, 361 pp.
       OCLC 5116671.

  98. Directorio de bibliotecas de la República Mexicana. México,
       DF: Secretaría de Educación Pública. Vols. for 1962–
       1970 issued by Departamento de Bibliotecas; 1979-- by
       Dirección General de Publicaciones y Bibliotecas,
       Secretaría de Educación Pública. 1962--. LC 80-641188.

  99. Directorio de bibliotecas de la República Mexicana. Suple-
       mento. 6. ed. México, DF: Secretaría de Educación
       Pública, 1980. xii, 588 pp. OCLC 8567554.

 100. García y García, J. Guía de archivos. [Instituciones con
       sede en el Distrito Federal]. México, DF: Instituto
       de Investigaciones Sociales, UNAM, 1972. 185 pp.
       LC 74-233262.

* 101. México, DF. Departamento de Bibliotecas. Directorio de
        bibliotecas de la República Mexicana. 2d ed. México,
        DF: El Departamento, 1965. 361 pp. LC 65-70955.

* 102. _____. Directorio de bibliotecas de la República
        Mexicana. 5th ed. México, DF: El El Departamento,
        1973. 335 pp. OCLC 2744069.

* 103. _____. Directorio de bibliotecas de la República
        Mexicana. 2 vols. 6th ed. México, DF: El Departa-
        mento, 1979. OCLC 6073587.

* 104. Ocampo, M. L., and S. Ortíz Vidales. Guía de las biblio-
        tecas en el Distrito Federal. México, DF: Talleres de
        El Nacional, 1943. 26 pp. LC 43-12720.

 105. Parsons, M. D., and R. A. Gordillo. Directorio de biblio-
       tecas de la Ciudad de México; una contribución a la VIII
       Feria Mexicana del Libro / Directory of Mexico City

Libraries, A Contribution to the VIII Mexican Book Fair. México, DF: Mexico City College Press, 1958. xix, 95 pp. LC 59-37909.

* 106. Peraza Sarausa, Fermín. Directorio de bibliotecas de México. Biblioteca del bibliotecario, 15. Havana: Ediciones Anuario Bibliográfico Cubano, 1958. 41 pp. LC 58-38830.

107. Quijano Solís, Alvaro. Directorio de unidades de información económica y social. México, DF: El Colegio de México, Biblioteca, 1977. (CCV)

108. _____. La situación de las unidades de información en el campo económico y social. Cuadernos de ABIESI, 5. México, DF: Asociación de Bibliotecarios de Instituciones de Enseñanza Superior e Investigación, 1977. 21 [30] leaves. (CCV)

Panama

109. Directorio de unidades de información agrícola en Panamá. Grupo Panameño de Información Agrícola, Instituto de Investigación Agropecuaria de Panamá. Panamá: GPIA, [1981]. ii, 58 leaves. OCLC 10328888.

* 110. Peraza Sarausa, Fermín. Directorio de bibliotecas de Panamá. Biblioteca de bibliotecario, 21. Havana: Anuario Bibliográfico Cubano, 1948. 34 pp. LC 49-16348.

Peru

* 111. Agrupación de Bibliotecas para la Integración de la Información Socio-Económica. Directorio de bibliotecas especializadas del Perú. Lima: 1972. (WVJ)

* 112. Guía de bibliotecas del Sistema Nacional de la Universidad Peruana, 1974. Comp. Elba Muñoz de Linares. Ser. Informaciones bibliotecológicas, 1. Lima: Consejo Nacional de la Universidad Peruana, Dirección de Evaluación de Universidades, Oficina de Evaluación, 1975. iv, 97 pp. LC 77-573632.

Puerto Rico

* 113. Alamo de Torres, Daisy. Directorio de bibliotecas de Puerto Rico. Rio Piedras, PR: Asociación Estudiantes Graduados de Bibliotecología, Universidad de Puerto Rico, 1979. 100 pp. LC 80-128849.

114. Directorio de unidades de información para el desarrollo,
      Estado Libre Asociado de Puerto Rico. Santiago:
      Centro Latinoamericano de Documentación, Económica y
      Social, Comisión Económica para América Latina, 1978.
      vii, 42 pp. LC 82-232775.

* 115. Pagán Jiménez, Neida. "Caribbean Library Resources in
      Puerto Rico." In Final Report and Working Papers
      of the Twenty-Fourth Seminar on the Acquisition of
      Latin American Library Materials. Los Angeles, CA,
      June 17-22, 1979. Madison, WI: SALALM, 1980.
      Pp. 193-198.

* 116. Sociedad de Bibliotecarios de Puerto Rico. Guía de
      bibliotecas de Puerto Rico. Josefina del Toro, ed.
      Rev. San Juan, PR: La Sociedad, 1971. 63 pp.
      OCLC 4348585.

Uruguay

* 117. Directorio de servicios de información y documentación en el
      Uruguay. Montevideo: Biblioteca Nacional, 1981.
      128 pp. OCLC 8160183.

* 118. Montevideo. Biblioteca del Poder Legislativo. Bibliotecas
      del Uruguay. Selección, textos y compilación, Maria
      Teresa Goicoechea de Linares, con la colaboración de
      Cristina O. de Pérez Olave y Lilian Fernández Citera.
      Serie de temas nacionales, 5. Montevideo: La Biblio-
      teca, 1978. 252 pp. LC 79-102436.

Venezuela

119. Bibliotecas de la Universidad Central de Venezuela. Caracas:
      Dirección de Bibliotecas, Información, Documentación y
      Publicaciones de la U.C.V., 1981. 39 pp. (AAJ)

120. Directorio de bibliotecas, centros de información, docu-
      mentación, análisis de información, bancos de datos en
      ingeniería, arquitectura y profesiones afines. Caracas:
      Biblioteca Central de Telecomunicaciones de la
      C.A.N.T.V., 1981. xxiii, 271 pp. LC 82-234840.

121. Directorio de bibliotecas de instituciones de educación
      superior en Venezuela. Equipo de Trabajo para la
      Creación de una Red de Educación Superior, comp.
      Caracas: [s.n., 198_?]. 17 leaves. (AAJ)

122. "Directorio de bibliotecas del Distrito Federal, de interés
      para los educadores." Información Educativa, 1:3
      (April-June, 1980), 18-25. (AAJ)

123. Farías, Rosa Carmen. Directorio de bibliotecas biomédicas venzolanas. Caracas: Sistema Nacional de Documentación e Información Biomédica, Biblioteca Humberto García Arocha, Instituto de Medicina Experimental, U.C.V., 1980. 57 pp. (AAJ)

124. García O., J. A. Guía de Bibliotecas de Venezuela. Caracas: [s.n.], 1969. 45 pp. (AAJ)

125. Instituto Autónomo Biblioteca Nacional y de Servicios de Bibliotecas Públicas, Coordinación Nacional de Redes Estadales. Directorio de bibliotecas públicas: Región Nor Oriental; Región Los Llanos; Región Central; Región Los Andes; Región Guayana; Región Centro Occidental; Región Insular; Región Zuliana. Caracas: El Instituto, [1983]. (AAJ)

126. Marín, Olivia. Directorio de bibliotecas venezolanas. Caracas: Universidad Central de Venezuela, Dirección de Bibliotecas, Información, Documentación y Publicaciones, Departamento de Orientación, Información y Documentación, 1973. 99 pp. LC 76-474325.

127. Primera, Nelly. Red de bibliotecas públicas del Estado Zulia. Caracas: Instituto Autónomo Biblioteca Nacional y de Servicios de Bibliotecas, 1983. (AAJ)

128. Red de información petrolera y petroquímica, directorio de bibliotecas y centros de información. Caracas: Reproducción Pequiven, 1980. 48 leaves. (AAJ)

129. Red de Información Socio-Económica. Directorio de REDINSE. Caracas: Red de Información Socio-Económica, 1974--. LC 75-644750.

130. Rojas Brunicelli, Sonia. Directorio de bibliotecas especializades en el área metropolitana. Caracas: Instituto Autónomo Biblioteca Nacional, Servicio de Información a la Comunidad, 1981. 27 leaves. (AAJ)

PROGRAM OF SUBSTANTIVE PANELS AND WORKSHOPS
SALALM XXIX

Chapel Hill, North Carolina
June 2-7, 1984

Saturday, June 2
    1-5 p.m.   Latin American Microform Project (LAMP) meeting

Sunday, June 3
    8 a.m.- 10 p.m.   Committee meetings

Monday, June 4
    9-10 a.m.   OPENING GENERAL SESSION

Presiding: John Hébert, President
Rapporteur: Charles Fineman
Local Arrangements: William D. Ilgen
                             Rafael Coutin

11 a.m.-1 p.m.   THEME PANEL

National Level Cooperation, Cooperative
Collection Development Programs, and the
Research Libraries Group

Presiding: Dan Hazen, Stanford University

Participants:
    Deborah L. Jakubs, Duke University
        RLG and the Conspectus
    Dan Hazen, Stanford University
        Review of Collection Development at
        Stanford University: A Practical Experience
    William D. Ilgen, University of North
    Carolina, Chapel Hill
        Tri-University Cooperation in Collection
        Development

Tuesday, June 5
    8:30-10 a.m.   THEME PANEL

Latin American Library Development, Collection
Development, and the Development of Latin
American Studies: An Historical Overview

Presiding: John Hébert, Library of Congress

Participants:
    Marietta D. Shepard, Bedford, Pennsylvania
        The Development of Library Collections
        in and out of Latin American
    Carlos Victor Penna, Tampa, Florida
        The Development of Latin American
        Libraries

Federico G. Gil, University of North Carolina, Chapel Hill
> The Development of Latin American Studies Programs in the United States

10:30 a.m.-12   THEME PANEL

Cooperative Collection Development in a Research Library

Presiding: William D. Ilgen, University of North Carolina, Chapel Hill

Participants:
Enrique Baloyra Herp, Director, Institute of Latin American Studies, University of North Carolina, Chapel Hill
> Social Sciences

María A. Salgado, Department of Literature, University of North Carolina, Chapel Hill
> Literature

Joseph Tulchin, Department of History, University of North Carolina, Chapel Hill
> History

1:30-3 p.m.   WORKSHOPS AND ROUNDTABLES

1. Primary Sources: Collection, Organization, and Integration into Bibliographic Instruction

Presiding: Sue K. Norman, Dickinson College

Participants:
Marilyn P. Whitmore, University of Pittsburgh
> Collection and Organization of Primary Materials

Thomas Niehaus, Tulane University
> Use of Tulane University's Photo Archive as a Primary Source

Tamara Brunnschweiler, Michigan State University
> Use of Cartographic Materials as Primary Sources

Peter Johnson, Princeton University
> Interviewing as a Primary Source

2. AACR2, the Library of Congress, and OCLC

Presiding: Gayle Williams, University of New Mexico

Participants:
Richard Ricard, Library of Congress
> AACR2 and the Library of Congress

David Zubatsky, OCLC
> OCLC and Cataloging

Donald Wisdom, Library of Congress
> Cataloging of Newspapers

3. Research Publications: Current and Future Projects

Participants:
Duane Bogenschneider, Research Publications
Research Publications: Current and Future
Projects
George Elmendorf, Nicaraguan National
Bibliography
Central American National Bibliographies:
Progress and Future Plans

Wednesday, June 6
10:30 a.m.-12   THEME PANEL

Latin American Legal Resources for the Social Scientist

Presiding: Igor I. Kavass, Director, Law Library,
Vanderbilt University

Participants:
Rubens Medina, Hispanic Law Division,
Library of Congress
Research Trends and Needs
Ellen G. Schaffer, Law School Library,
Georgetown University
Acquisition of Legal Materials
Selma Cervetti de Rodríguez, Inter-American
Development Bank
Reference and Bibliographic Sources

1:30-3 p.m.   WORKSHOPS AND ROUNDTABLES

1. Foreign Acquisition Field Trips

Presiding: Nelly S. González, University of Illinois

Participants:
Thomas Niehaus, Tulane University
Buying Trips to Latin America: Ideas and
Suggestions
Patricia E. Noble, University of London
Acquisition Field Trips: A
British Perspective
Walter V. Brem, Jr., Arizona State University
(with Nelly S. González and Heidi Hanson)
Uses of Foreign Acquisition Field Trips

2. AACR2 and Special Format Materials

Presiding: Cecilia Sercan

Participants:
Eugene Ferguson, Library of Congress
Microform Cataloging
John Schroeder, Library of Congress
Map Cataloging
Jackie Dooley, Library of Congress
Print Cataloging

3. Faxon, the LINKS System, and Periodical
   Subscriptions for Latin American Periodicals

   Participants:
   Barbara G. Valk, University of California,
   Los Angeles
   Kit Kennedy, Faxon Subscription Service

4. Collection Development in the Eastern Caribbean

   Participant:
   Alan Moss, University of the West Indies,
   Cave Hill, Barbados

Thursday, June 7
9-11 a.m.   BUSINESS MEETING AND
                          CLOSING GENERAL SESSION

President: John Hébert
Rapporteur: Charles Fineman

Officers' Reports:
   Executive Secretary: Suzanne Hodgman
   Treasurer: David Lee

Reports of the Executive Board Committees:
   Constitution and By-Laws: Sara de Mundo Lo
   Editorial Board: Barbara G. Valk
   Awards Panel: Peter Johnson
   Membership: Mina Jane Grothey
   Finance: Laura Gutiérrez-Witt
   Nominations: Peter de la Garza
   Acquisitions: Robert McNeil
   Bibliography: Paula Covington
   Library Operations and Services: Iliana Sonntag
   Interlibrary Cooperation: Carl Deal
   Official Publications: Gene Wiemers

Special Reports:
   Latin American Microform Project (LAMP)
   Hispanic American Periodicals Index (HAPI)

Special Remembrance: Jane Garner

Resolutions
Introduction of New Officers
Introduction of New Committee Chairs: Dan Hazen
Other Business
Adjournment of the Business Meeting

CLOSURE OF SALALM XXIX

ACRONYMS

ABIESI	Asociación de Bibliotecarios de Instituciones de Enseñanza Superior e Investigaciones (Mexico)
AID	Agency for International Development (U.S.A.)
ALADI	Asociación Latinoamericana de Integración
ALIDE	Asociación Latinoamericana de Instituciones Financieros de Desarrollo
ARL	Association of Research Libraries (U.S.A.)
ARPEL	Asistencia Recíproca Petrolera Estatal Latinoamericana
CDU	Classificação Decimal Universal
CEPAL	Comisión Económica para América Latina y el Caribe
CIRMA	Centro de Investigaciones Regionales de Mesoamérica
CLADES	Centro Latinoamericano de Documentación Económica y Social
CONICYT	Consejo Nacional de Investigaciones Científicas y Tecnológicas (Costa Rica)
FAO	Food and Agriculture Organization of the United Nations
FID	Federación Internacional de Documentación
IADB	Inter-American Development Bank
IBBD	Instituto Brasileiro de Bibliografia y Documentação
IBEDOC	International Bureau, Educational Documentation
ILL	Inter-Library Loan
INTAL	Instituto para la Integración de América Latina
LAFTA	Latin American Free Trade Association
LARR	Latin American Research Review
LASA	Latin American Studies Association (U.S.A.)
LC	Library of Congress (U.S.A.)
MARI	Middle American Research Institute, Tulane University (U.S.A.)
MLA	Modern Language Association (U.S.A.)
NCIP	North American Collections Inventory Project
NDEA	National Defense Education Act (U.S.A.)
NDFL	National Defense and Foreign Languages Act (U.S.A.)
NUCMC	National Union Catalog of Manuscript Collections
OAS	Organization of American States
OCLC	Online Computer Library Center (U.S.A.)

OEA	Organización de Estados Americanos
OIT	Organización Internacional de Trabajo
PCR	Primary Collecting Responsibility (Research Libraries Group)
REDINSE	Red de Información Socio-Economica (Venezuela)
RLG	Research Libraries Group, Inc. (U.S.A.)
RLIN	Research Libraries Information Network (U.S.A.)
SLA	Special Library Association (U.S.A.)
SCOLAS	Southern Council on Latin American Studies (U.S.A.)
SECOLAS	Southeastern Council on Latin American Studies (U.S.A.)
UCV	Universidad Central de Venezuela
UFMG	Universidade Federal de Minas Gerais
UNAM	Universidad Nacional Autonoma de México
UNESCO	United Nations Educational, Scientific, and Cultural Organization
UWIDITE	University of the West Indies Distance Teaching Experiment
WILIP	West Indian Legislative Indexing Project

ABOUT THE AUTHORS

WALTER V. BREM, JR. was the Iberoamerican Area Specialist at the Hayden Library, Arizona State University, at the time his paper was presented. He is currently Assistant Head of Public Services at the Bancroft Library, University of California, Berkeley.

SELMA CERVETTI DE RODRIGUEZ was Law Librarian at the Inter-American Development Bank in Washington, DC, at the time she presented her paper. A graduate of the School of Library Sciences, University of Uruguay, she is currently working in the Inter-American Development Bank's office in Montevideo.

FEDERICO G. GIL is Kennan Professor of Political Science Emeritus, the University of North Carolina, Chapel Hill.

NELLY S. GONZALEZ is Latin American Bibliographer and Assistant Professor of Library Administration, University of Illinois Library, Urbana-Champaign.

HEIDI HANSON is Head of the Catalog Maintenance Section, Cataloging Department, at the Ohio State University Libraries.

WILLIAM D. ILGEN is Latin American and Iberian Resources Bibliographer at the Davis Library, University of North Carolina, Chapel Hill.

DEBORAH L. JAKUBS was associated with the Research Libraries Group, Inc., Stanford, California, at the time she presented her paper. She is currently the Ibero-American Bibliographer at Duke University.

IGOR I. KAVASS is Professor of Law and Director of Legal Information at the Alyne Queener Massey Law Library, Vanderbilt University. He served as President of the International Association of Law Libraries from 1977 to 1983 and is currently Chairman of the Board of Trustees, International Association of Law Libraries.

CELIA LEYTE-VIDAL was Monograph Cataloger at the Perkins Library, Duke University, until her retirement in 1985.

JESUS LEYTE-VIDAL was the Ibero-American Librarian at the Perkins Library, Duke University, until his retirement in 1985.

RUBENS MEDINA has served since 1981 as Chief of the Hispanic Law Division of the Library of Congress. He received his legal training in Paraguay and at the University of Wisconsin and is co-author of Nomenclature and Hierarchy: Basic Latin American Legal Sources.

ALAN MOSS is Acquisitions Librarian at the Main Library, University of the West Indies, Cave Hill campus, Bridgetown, Barbados.

THOMAS NIEHAUS is Director of the Latin American Library, Tulane University.

PATRICIA E. NOBLE is Librarian for the Latin American Collection, Senate House, University of London.

MARIA A. SALGADO is Professor of Spanish at the University of North Carolina, Chapel Hill.

ELLEN G. SCHAFFER is International and Foreign Law Librarian at the Georgetown University Law Center.

BARBARA G. VALK is Coordinator of Bibliographic Development at the UCLA Latin American Center. She is Editor of the Hispanic American Periodicals Index and BorderLine: Bibliography of the U.S.-Mexican Borderlands.

MARILYN P. WHITMORE was University Archivist at the Hillman Library, University of Pittsburgh, at the time she presented her paper. She is now Coordinator of Instruction at the Hillman Library.